Stumpwork Embroidery

Techniques, projects and pure inspiration

Kay & Michael Dennis

SEARCH PRESS

First published in 2014

Search Press Limited
Wellwood, North Farm Road,
Tunbridge Wells, Kent TN2 3DR

Based on the following books published by Search Press:
Beginner's Guide to Stumpwork by Kay Dennis, 2001
Stumpwork Figures by Kay & Michael Dennis, 2006
Stumpwork Seasons by Kay & Michael Dennis, 2007

Text copyright © Kay Dennis and Michael Dennis 2014
www.kaydennis.co.uk

Photographs by Charlotte de la Bédoyère, Search Press Studios;
and Roddy Paine Photographic Studio
Photographs and design copyright © Search Press Ltd

ISBN: 978-1-78221-102-0

Suppliers
If you have difficulty in obtaining any of the materials and
equipment mentioned in this book, please visit the Search Press
website for details of suppliers:
www.searchpress.com

Alternatively, to obtain materials and equipment, including
a full-sized copy of the seasons template (see page 115),
via the authors' mail-order service, visit:
www.kaydennis.co.uk

Publishers' note
All the step-by-step photographs in this book feature
the authors, Kay and Michael Dennis, demonstrating
stumpwork techniques. No models have been used.

Acknowledgements

*To all our friends and students who continue to support
and encourage us. To Neil and Patricia Wood of
Mulberry Silks; Jane and Sarah Jane of
Threads of Amersham; Wendy James of Mace & Nairn;
Jean Oliver of Oliver Twists; Bob Weston for the needlelace
pillow stand and pillow on page 40; and Rebecca Balchin
for the fairy designs on pages 3, 72 and 82–89.*

*Special thanks must go to Lotti and Roz at Search Press,
and especially our Editor, Katie, who has shown unending
patience as we constantly change our minds about the
content of the embroidery.*

*We would not have been able to write this book without
those people who taught Kay embroidery, needlelace and
stumpwork. Thanks go to Cathy Barley, Pat Gibson,
Doreen Holmes and Denise Montgomery, with special
thanks to Roy and Barbara Hirst.*

*We would like to thank several people who helped us with
the designs in this book – Kay's football-loving cousin, Hazel,
who advised us on team colours for the footballer (see page
67), and our friend Barbara who taught Kay how to make
clothes with a sewing machine. The only person we cannot
thank is Kay's dear dad who passed away twenty years
ago, and who provided the inspiration for the fisherman
(see pages 90–100).*

*This book is in recognition of all our students who constantly
present us with new challenges – challenges that fuel our
inspiration and enthusiasm for discovering new and exciting
initiatives in stumpwork.*

Contents

Introduction

Stumpwork dates from the seventeenth century and, like all seventeenth-century embroiderers, I was introduced to embroidery at an early age. My great aunt taught me the easy stitches, then, at school, my teachers encouraged me in a subject I enjoyed and excelled in.

In the late 1960s I attended a textile course, where I was introduced to the technique of needlelace. I only made a small leaf shape, but I enjoyed making it so much that I decided to explore the techniques further. Although I still practised embroidery, I began to love needlelace and all its possibilities.

Two decades on I found stumpwork, which meant I could combine my two passions – embroidery and needlelace – bliss! My stumpwork tutors, Barbara and Roy Hirst, not only taught me the techniques but instilled in me a love and appreciation of this complex but fascinating style of embroidery. I began teaching needlelace in 1984 and stumpwork in 1994, and my enthusiasm for both these crafts is still strong – I just love stitching.

In recent years my work has changed, largely due to my teaching activities; I have explored new threads and materials, and different ways of using them. Although I still like to embroider in a traditional style, my work has taken on a more contemporary appearance. I tried using a sewing machine, but hand stitching is my first love.

Traditional stumpwork is small, intricate and, sometimes, frustrating to make. But – once hooked – you will look at embroidery differently, and you may even find that flat needlework looks uninteresting.

Stumpwork is sometimes confused with the Elizabethan style of padded embroidery. Both types of work are raised, but the styles are completely different. The Elizabethan style generally has scrolled patterns, in the form of coiling stems, with flowers and fruits, whereas the later stumpwork embroideries are more picturesque.

Stumpwork is currently enjoying a revival, due largely to Barbara Hirst who, having discovered this delightful form of embroidery in 1980, started to teach and demonstrate it around the world. It grows ever-popular with embroiderers and lacemakers alike, who use both traditional materials and the extensive range of modern ones. A typical modern stumpwork embroidery contains flat, padded and freestanding embroidery, and slips (small pieces of needlework made on separate pieces of fabric).

Stumpwork is not as alarming as it might first appear. In this book, I have included projects that even someone new to embroidery can achieve with ease. I show you, step by step, how to make and use different types of padding, and the embroidery and needlelace stitches commonly used in stumpwork. All of the embroidery stitches used in the book are illustrated in a stitch library at the back of the book for easy reference. When you get used to the stitches and techniques, try to develop your own ideas by experimenting with modern materials.

Various materials are used to enhance stumpwork embroideries, including modelling clay, balsa wood, wires and buttons, and this is where Michael's expertise comes into play. Michael is responsible for designing and making the non-stitched objects that appear in many of the designs, leaving me free to do all of the embroidery. Michael also produced all of the drawings and diagrams in the book.

This book will help and encourage all embroiderers who like to stitch by hand and I hope it will enthuse those who have never attempted stumpwork before. Given a little guidance and some basic equipment, stumpwork is a skill any embroiderer can acquire. The real joy of this technique is designing and creating an original and unique embroidery that will be treasured for years to come.

Finally, I would like to pass on a few tips that I found out about by accident! Put a cloth over your embroidery when you are not stitching to keep it clean; wash your hands before doing any embroidery and, most important of all, keep tea and coffee away from the work. I once tripped over an extension cable stretched across my workroom, spilt a cup of coffee and ruined several months' embroidery work!

Kay Dennis

History

Dictionaries define stumpwork as: 'elaborate raised embroidery of the fifteenth to seventeenth centuries using various materials, and raised by stumps of wood or pads of wool'. In the seventeenth century it was called raised or embossed work. Later, it became known as 'embroidery on the stump', and the term 'stumpwork' was first used in the nineteenth century. We are not sure how the term came about, but it was probably because of the small stumps of wood used to raise parts of the embroidery.

Towards the end of the seventeenth century, this highly elaborate, intricate and decorative form of raised and padded embroidery became popular in Britain. It was used to decorate caskets, boxes, mirror frames, panels, book covers and pin cushions. Although new to England, a similar style of embroidery had been worked by professional European embroiderers for over a century.

Embroidery was an essential part of the education of young ladies of the time, and they worked samplers in canvaswork, whitework, needlelace and beadwork. The samplers were often limited in design so, having mastered the basic skills, the ladies wanted to use them in a less restrictive way. Imagine their delight in selecting materials, threads and patterns, then working something new and exciting.

Embroiderers did not create their own designs; they had an endless source of material in contemporary pattern books, woodcuts and engravings.

British stumpwork box, circa 1650, gifted to the Embroiderers' Guild Museum Collection, Hampton Court Palace, by Miss Hester Clough.

JULIA HEDGECOE

8

Enlarged detail taken from the stumpwork opposite.

Having chosen a pattern, the embroiderer would employ a professional printmaker to paint or print the design on to a silk or satin background. A typical example of period stumpwork would include human figures, mythological figures, animals, castles, flowers, fruits and insects, filling every space. No attention was paid to scale: the motifs were often disproportionate in size to each other.

The embroiderers would possibly have worked from kits containing most of the materials they needed, including small, ready-formed pieces of wood (probably boxwood) in the shape of fruit, hands and heads to be covered with stitching.

Other materials would include gold threads, dyed silk and chenille threads and fabrics, metal purl, beads, pearls, semi-precious stones, hair and feathers. Wires and vellum, bound with silk, were used to provide further textural and decorative detail.

On completion the embroidery would be sent to a cabinetmaker to be mounted on to a casket or mirror frame.

Materials and equipment

All the materials used in stumpwork are generally available from good needlework shops. Mail-order outlets, which advertise in needlework magazines, and the internet are also good sources of materials.

Threads

A very wide range of threads can be used in stumpwork – cotton, silk, metallic, synthetic and wool, all in hundreds of different colours and textures, and each creating a different result. With experience, you will learn how to select the correct thread for the effect you want to achieve. Fine threads work best in stumpwork, for example 100/3 silks or one strand of six-stranded cotton. Space-dyed threads can be used to create interesting finishes – we prefer hand-dyed to machine-dyed types as the latter can produce a less attractive, stripey effect. Always use the best threads you can afford – some of the cheaper stranded cottons shred and fluff easily, giving an untidy appearance to your embroidery.

We have used mainly **stranded cottons**, **stranded silks** and **100/3 silk threads** in this book; silks give a lovely sheen to the stitches and are especially good for flowers and insects. The only other threads used are a **bouclé wool**, **fine tapestry wool** and **metallic thread**. A tubular metallic thread known as **bullion** has been used for the dragonfly's body on page 127. **Sewing cotton** is used for work that is not going to be visible on the finished embroidery, for example for securing pads and couching down the cordonnet threads, as shown on page 38.

Needles & pins

Always use a needle that is appropriate for the purpose. It should pass through the fabric easily, and it should have an eye large enough to take the thread you are using comfortably, but not so big that the thread keeps falling out. The following types of needle are ideal for stumpwork: **embroidery needles** are used for all embroidery stitches where the threads pass through the fabric. They have long eyes and sharp points. **Sharps needles** are good for all general sewing. **Ballpoint needles** are used for making needlelace and for surface stitching, and a **darning needle** to help pass wires through the background fabrics.

Lace pins, which are similar to **dressmakers' pins** but with a longer and thinner shank, are ideal for holding small pieces of needlelace in position before sewing them in place. **Berry-head** and **flower-head pins** are used for securing larger pieces of embroidery.

Kay's pincushion, showing the range of needles and pins she uses.

Basic sewing equipment

A **thimble** is especially useful when sewing through leather and other tough materials. **Tweezers** are used for handling very small pieces of embroidery, such as needlelace and slips, and for removing small trimmings of thread. A **crochet hook** is used in needlelace to help lay the cordonnet. Always use sharp **scissors** – a large pair for cutting fabrics, a general-purpose pair for cutting paper, wire, etc., and a small, very sharp-pointed pair for cutting threads. It is advisable to buy the best you can afford; a good pair of scissors is an embroiderer's best friend and, if well cared for, will last a long time.

Background fabrics

Two layers of a plain background fabric, strong enough to support the sometimes heavily padded and wired elements, should be used for stumpwork. Medium- or lightweight **calico** has been used as the background fabric for the embroideries in this book, with a layer of medium-weight calico underneath. Lightweight calico, which folds more easily, is best for making slips and stuffed pads for faces.

Some elements, such as the ferns and the squirrel's tail in the seasons project (page 110), have been embroidered on **silk organza**. Because it is very sheer, the embroidered elements can be cut out, and any surplus fabric will not be visible against the calico background.

Silk chiffon is a soft, floaty fabric that can be used as the top layer on water; when painted it gives a rippled effect. Unpainted chiffon placed over a painted background will give it a misty appearance. To give a rough texture, for example to the grassy area at the base of the seasons embroidery, **silk noil** has been used. The freestanding daffodil petals on page 135 have been embroidered on **watersoluble fabric**. It is tough enough for hand embroidery, but can be dissolved away from the stitching, which can then be sewn on to the background fabric.

TIP

Binding the inner ring of an embroidery hoop will help keep the fabric taut. Use strips of cotton sheeting cut on the bias.

Frames

Mounting the background fabrics in a frame will help keep a good tension on your work. **Circular embroidery frames** or **hoops** are available in many sizes and are very easy to use. The background fabric is supported between two concentric rings, the outer one of which can be adjusted using a screw clamp. **Silk frames** and pins are used for stretching fabric before it is painted.

Other fabrics and materials

Polyester toy stuffing has been used to fill three-dimensional elements. It pulls out to almost single strands and can be pushed into the smallest of spaces. Quilters' wadding is not suitable for stumpwork. **Interfacing** is a fabric stiffener available in different thicknesses – a firm, heavy-weight grade has been used throughout this book for raising flat surfaces. Interfacing can be coloured with fabric paints. **Felt** can also be used for padding. Layers can be built up to give a domed appearance to the shape, or by stuffing a single layer of felt with toy stuffing. Use a wool felt, as acrylic felt is too rigid for small pieces of stumpwork.

Cotton moulds are available from craft and hobby shops, and are ideal for making apples, oranges, etc. They should be painted before being covered with thread. **Balsa wood** is a good alternative to cotton moulds; it is a very soft wood that can be sculpted with a craft knife.

We have used **horsehair** or **fishing line** to strengthen the outlines of freestanding needlelace shapes, and incorporated **fine copper wire** under the top stitching of some of the pieces of needlelace and around the freestanding embroidery to allow them to be bent into shape. **Paper-covered wire** wrapped with stranded cotton has been used to form flower stalks and birds' legs.

To introduce different textures into the embroideries, a very soft **gloving leather** has been used for some of the birds' bodies; **balsa wood** and **lime wood** for the log cabin and the fence (see pages 130–131; 137–138); and **cotton fibres** for the snow (page 129).

Painting equipment

We have used **watersoluble crayons** and **fabric paints** to colour background fabrics, interfacing pads, cotton moulds, fabric slips and other materials. They are also useful for adding eyebrows and nostrils to faces (see the Figures section on page 66). **Acrylic paints** have also been used, for example for the heron's markings on pages 154–155. Fabric and acrylic paints are applied using small and medium-sized **paintbrushes**; if watersoluble crayons are used, the coloured background is then painted over with a large paintbrush dampened with clean water to blend the paint. It is useful to have some **kitchen roll** to hand for mopping up spills and removing excess paint.

Other equipment

Though not essential, a **lightbox** makes it easier to transfer your designs on to fabric. **Pressed-paper egg boxes**, when cut, shaped and painted, make realistic rocks, such as those surrounding the pond in the lower half of the seasons picture (page 136), and **thin card**, such as tissue-box card, is ideal for making templates for arms and legs. **PVA glue** is used to secure the threads when wrapping wire and to glue balsa wood and lime wood together. **Cocktail sticks** are used to push toy stuffing into a felt pad, and to manipulate very small elements. You'll need a **heavy-duty craft knife**, a **small craft knife** and a **cutting mat** for cutting tough materials, such as balsa wood and lime wood; a **drawing pen**, **pencil** and **eraser** for sketching on to paper and for transferring patterns and templates on to **tracing paper**; a **gold gel pen** or **gold acrylic paint** for outlining the templates on the background fabric; **self-adhesive, transparent plastic** to form the protective layer on needlelace pads; and **surgical tape** or **masking tape** to pad out limbs, such as the frog's thighs on page 159, under the needlelace. A **stiletto** is a sharp, pointed tool useful for making small holes in fabric. **Air-drying clay**, though not essential, is useful for creating special shapes, such as flowerpots. Finally, embellishments in the form of **small buttons** and **beads** are useful for decorating your embroideries, and for making tiny animals' eyes.

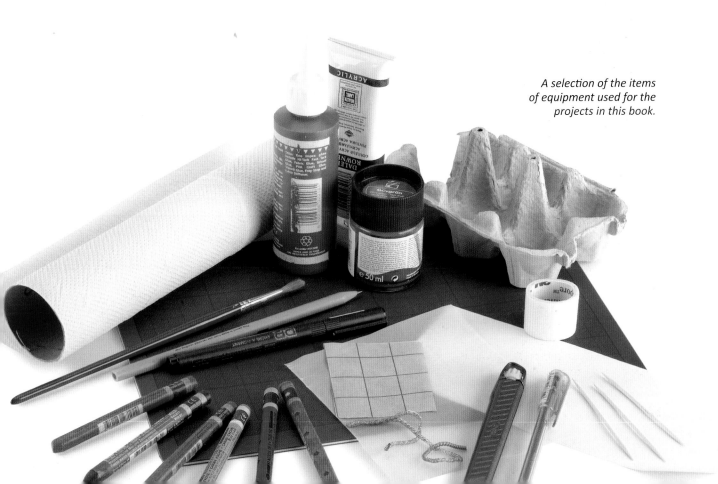

A selection of the items of equipment used for the projects in this book.

Getting started

In this section, we cover a few simple tasks that must be performed before you start to work on an embroidery. First, you have to work up your design and create a full-size paper pattern. Then you must transfer it to the background fabric, prepare your embroidery hoop and mount the background fabric in it.

Creating a design

As a beginner, you will probably want to start by copying the designs from this book. Soon, however, you will want to create your own. So, where do you start? Well, there are lots of sources of inspiration.

Children's colouring books, magazines, greetings cards and postcards, for example, often have images that could – with a little imagination – be turned into a stumpwork embroidery. The law of copyright says that you cannot make exact copies of other people's designs without their permission, but there is nothing wrong with adapting them.

When you go out and about, take a small sketchbook with you; even if you cannot sketch well, a simple drawing with notes of colours that you see will help remind you of a design idea.

Alternatively, you can get some very good results with a small, point-and-shoot camera. Shots of the whole scene, as well as details, could be useful in the future.

Your family and friends will soon get used to you taking the most unusual pictures!

Try to find a natural subject with a shape or colour range that appeals to you – be it a flower, a fungus, a rock, a bird, an insect or even some fruit – then make lots of sketches or take several photographs.

When you have your source material, start to work up a design. Use a photocopier to enlarge or reduce different images to the same scale. Break a complex subject into individual shapes – the calyx, petals, stalks and leaves of a flower, for example – and try to simplify the shape without losing its identity. Try putting some of the shapes together; a fungus growing on a tree-stump, or an insect sitting on a flower.

Gradually, you will start to look at the world around you in a different way. Something will catch your eye and you will find yourself saying: 'How can I recreate that in stumpwork?'

When you have chosen your subject, make a pencil sketch, simplifying the shapes as much as possible.

Preparing the background fabric

When you are happy with your design, make a full-size paper pattern. Cut the fabric to size, remembering to add an allowance for framing the finished work, fold it to find its centre, then mark this point with a pin.

Place the pin over the centre of the paper pattern and transfer the design on to the fabric. Shown below is the traditional method of using a fine brush and gold fabric paint to draw outlines on to fabric but alternatively you could use a gold gel pen. You only need to transfer the basic outlines of the design, as all detail will be covered by stitches. Do not transfer the outlines of any freestanding elements of your embroidery, or they will show. When the paint is completely dry, use an iron to 'heat set' it.

Hoop frames are more than adequate for the projects in this book. Use hoops 5cm (2in) larger all round than the design. If you have to use a small frame with a large design, work the design area by area.

Most hoop frames have a tightening mechanism, but the embroidery fabric can still slip. Binding the inner ring with strips of cotton sheeting cut on the bias will keep the fabric taut.

Centre the design over the bound inner ring then clamp it with the outer one. Fine fabrics, such as silk or lightweight calico, will not support the weight of stumpwork on their own, so mount a piece of medium-weight calico behind these.

Remove the fabric from the frame when you finish a needle-work session; if the fabric is left in the frame for long periods of time, the rings may cause marks which can be difficult to remove.

Fold the fabric in half, then in half again to find the centre point. Mark this with a dressmaker's pin.

Open up the fabric, then centre it over the design. A lightbox or a sunny window will help you position it.

Use a fine brush and gold fabric paint to transfer the outlines of the design from the pattern on to the fabric.

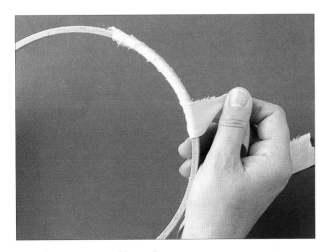

Bind the inner ring of hoop frames to help keep the fabric taut.

Place the fabric over the inner ring, press the outer ring over the top, pull the fabric taut, then tighten the clamp.

Embroidery techniques

In this chapter, we take you through the basic techniques of embroidered stumpwork. This sampler (shown right) includes five projects and some smaller, filler designs. Individual projects would make delightful embroideries on their own, and could be framed to make the perfect gift for someone special. The smaller designs, the patterns for which are included at the back of the book, could, for example, be used to decorate the lid of a box.

Each project is complete with step-by-step instructions to show you how to use different padding and raising techniques, and how to work the different stitches used to embroider it.

Note that all of the embroidery stitches shown here and in subsequent sections of the book are illustrated in the stitch library on pages 173–175.

Flowing Flowers

The padding used for the raised leaves and petals of this floral design are made from heavy-weight interfacing. This is quite stiff, making it ideal for the crisp edges of leaves and petals. It also makes satin stitch easier to work as it helps guide the needle passing through the background fabric. It's best to paint the interfacing to match the thread colour so that the eye is not distracted by any white peeping through the stitches. Interfacing accepts fabric paint easily, but let it dry overnight before using it.

Satin stitch covers all the leaves and flowers, stem stitch is used for the flower stalks, and turkey knot stitch forms the raised body of the butterfly. The wings of the butterfly, which stand proud of the surface, are worked in long and short stitch over wire couched down on a separate piece of fabric.

Materials
- Embroidery hoop
- Medium-weight calico
- Scissors
- Fabric paint and brush
- Heavyweight interfacing
- Tracing paper and pencil
- Sewing thread
- Six-stranded cotton
- No. 7 embroidery needle
- Dressmakers' pins
- Fine wire
- Stiletto

Full-size pattern. Use gold fabric paint or gold gel pen to transfer the outlines on to the background fabric. The wings of the butterfly stand proud of the surface, so do not transfer these. The petals coloured in pink are not padded, and the arrows on the other petals indicate the direction of the satin stitches.

Preparing the padding

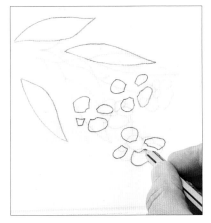

1 Transfer the outlines of the three leaves and the twelve petals shown here on to tracing paper, then cut out each shape. To avoid confusion, keep the groups of petals together until you are ready to use them.

2 Use a green fabric paint to colour a piece of interfacing (the area must be large enough to cut out the three leaves).

3 Pin a tracing-paper leaf shape to the dry, coloured interfacing, then cut out the shape.

Stab stitch

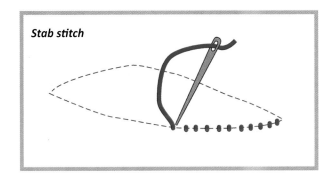

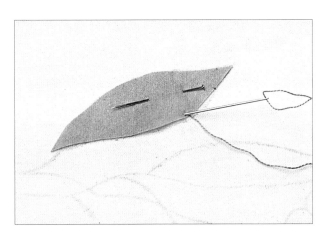

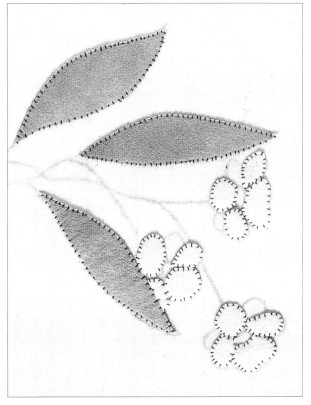

4 Pin the shape within its gold outline, then using a matching thread, stab stitch the leaf shape to the background fabric.

5 Cut out the other two leaves from the coloured interfacing, and the twelve petal shapes from white interfacing, then secure all the shapes to the background fabric using stab stitch.

19

Working the stalks

Stem stitch is used to work all the flower stalks. Use a No. 7 embroidery needle and one strand of six-stranded cotton thread. Work the longest stalks first, starting at the flower head or leaf end, then work the shorter stalks, blending them into the long ones.

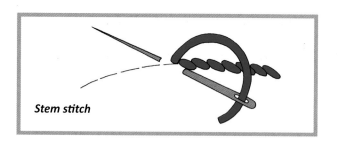

Stem stitch

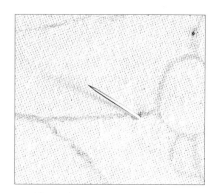

1 Bring the needle and thread up through the fabric approximately 6mm (¼in) from the start point of the stalk.

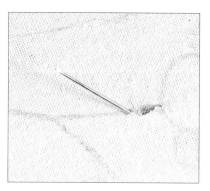

2 Take the needle down at the start point, then bring it back up again about 3mm (⅛in) beyond the first stitch.

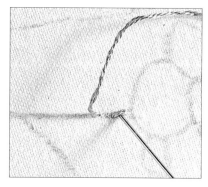

3 Now take the needle down through the fabric, approximately halfway along the first stitch.

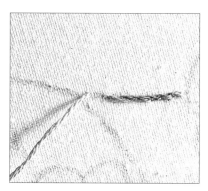

4 Bring the needle back up 3mm (⅛in) beyond the second stitch, then back down halfway along the second stitch. Continue working stitches until the stalk is complete.

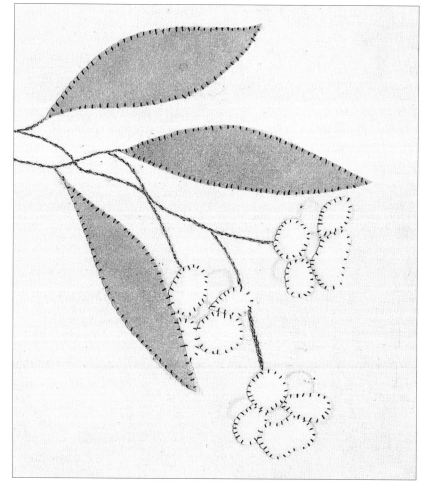

All stem-stitch stalks completed.

Working the leaves and petals

The leaves and petals are all embroidered in satin stitch using a No. 7 embroidery needle and one strand of six-stranded cotton.

Make the first stitch across the middle of the shape, work out to one side, then go back to the middle and work the other side.

The pink shapes on the diagram (see page 18) are not raised, and should be embroidered before working on the raised petals. Work the stitches from the centre of the flower outwards, generally in the direction of the arrows shown on the diagram.

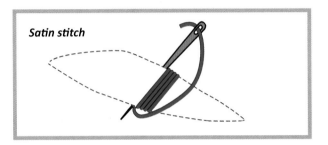

Satin stitch

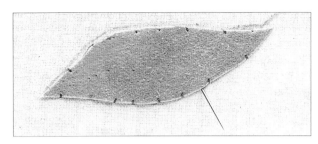

1 Bring the needle up through the fabric, one-third of the way along one side of the leaf shape.

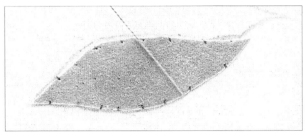

2 Take the thread diagonally across the shape, hold it flat, then take the needle down through the fabric where the thread crosses the edge of the padding.

3 Bring the needle up at the right-hand side of the thread on the bottom edge of the padding, take it across the leaf, parallel to the first stitch, then back down through the fabric again. Continue working across the leaf shape.

4 When you have covered the right-hand side of the shape, work another series of satin stitches from the centre out to the left-hand side. Work the other leaves in a similar way. If worked carefully, satin stitch creates a wonderful sheen across the shape.

All satin stitches completed. Note that the centre of each flower head is filled with French knots (see page 30).

21

Working the butterfly

The body of the butterfly, which completes this project, is worked in turkey knot stitch, using a No. 7 embroidery needle and two strands of six-stranded cotton. The resulting loops are trimmed off to create a fluffy raised area.

The wings are worked on a separate piece of calico. Fine wire formers are couched on to the fabric, then the enclosed shapes are worked with long and short stitches. These stitches are worked with one strand of six-stranded cotton.

For clarity, the step-by-step photographs for making the wings do not include the embroidered body.

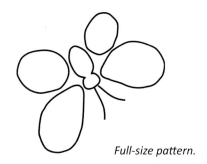

Full-size pattern.

Turkey knot stitch

This stitch produces rows of secured loops, which can then be trimmed to create a fluffy pile.

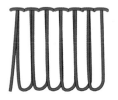

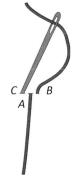

1. Insert the needle through the fabric at A, leaving a tail of thread on the surface. Bring the needle up at B, then down at C; pull the thread tight to make a small securing stitch.

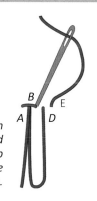

2. Bring the needle back up at A, then insert it at D, leaving a loop of thread on the surface. Bring the needle up at E, then down at B; again, pull the thread tight to make a securing stitch.

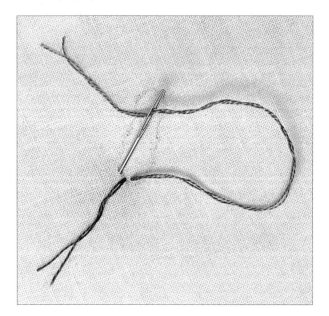

1 Starting at the bottom of the body, make the first knot leaving a short tail of thread on the surface.

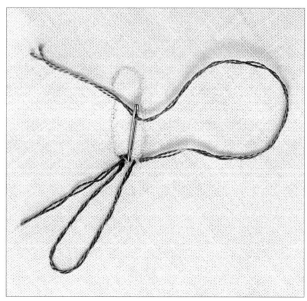

2 Tighten the knot, then, leaving a short loop on the surface, make another knot to one side.

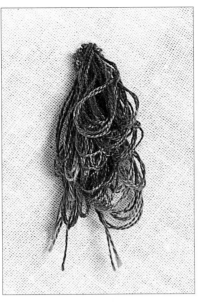

3 Take the thread across the back of the fabric, then bring it up just above the first row of knots. Make another row of knots, then, repeating this step, work up the body shape.

4 Continue making rows of knots until the body shape is completely filled with knots.

5 Use a sharp pair of scissors to trim off the loops to create a rounded fluffy pile.

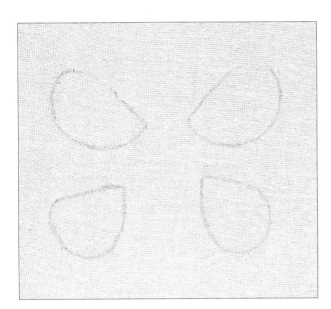

6 Transfer the outline of the four wings on to a piece of lightweight calico with gold fabric paint or gel pen, leaving space for cutting out each wing. Cut lengths of fine wire to fit the contour of each wing. Allow for two 25mm (1in) tails to support the wings when they are sewn on to the body.

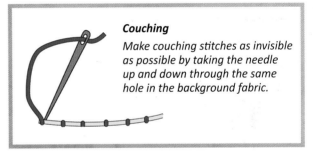

Couching
Make couching stitches as invisible as possible by taking the needle up and down through the same hole in the background fabric.

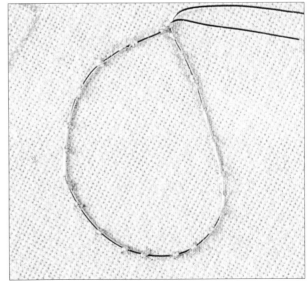

7 Couch the wire over the gold outlines.

Long and short stitch

On the second and subsequent rows of stitches, take the thread down through the end of the stitch on the previous row. This practice will give a very smooth finish to the stitches.

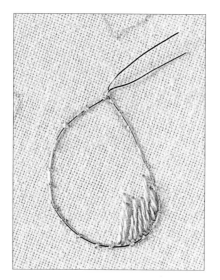

8 Starting at the right hand edge of the wing shape, use one strand of six-stranded cotton and a No. 7 embroidery needle to make a series of long and short stitches alternately across the shape.

9 On the next and subsequent rows, bring the needle and thread up a short distance away from the first short stitch of the previous row, then take the thread through the end of this stitch and back into the background fabric.

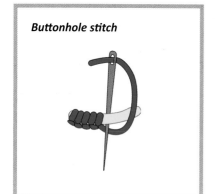

Buttonhole stitch

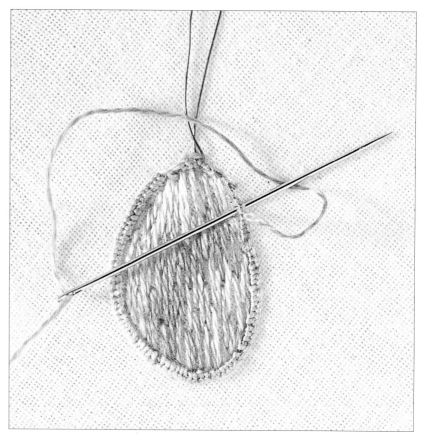

10 When the wing shape is completely filled with long and short stitch, work a hem of buttonhole stitches over the wire. Start at the base of the wing and work right round the shape. Do not cut off the excess thread as this will be used to secure the wing to the body shape.

11 Cut round the outside edge, as close as possible to the buttonhole stitches.

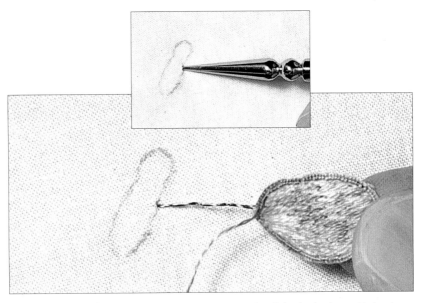

12 Use a stiletto to make a small hole in the side of the body shape. Twist the wire tails together, then push them through the hole to the back of the fabric. Take the loose length of thread through the same hole.

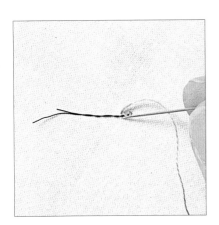

13 On the back of the fabric, fold the wire tail down the length of the body shape, then oversew it to secure it to the fabric. Repeat with the other three wings.

The finished embroidery.

Acorns

Felt, padded out with toy stuffing, is used to create the rounded appearance of the acorns in this project. The stalks are embroidered in stem stitch (see page 20), the leaves and the basic acorn shapes are worked in satin stitch (see page 21), then the tip of each acorn is finished with a small French knot (see page 30). Finally, the acorn cups are worked in Ceylon stitch, the texture of which is perfect for depicting the knobbly surface of the acorn cups.

Materials
• Embroidery hoop
• Medium-weight calico
• Scissors
• Fabric paint and brush
• Tracing paper and pencil
• Felt for padding
• Toy stuffing
• Cocktail stick
• Sewing thread
• Six-stranded cotton
• No. 7 embroidery needle

Stuffing the felt padding

Felt is a versatile padding material that can be stuffed to create rounded shapes for oversewing. Use a good quality fine felt, and select a colour that is compatible with the embroidery threads.

Cut the felt shapes so that they sit just inside the gold outline on the fabric. Stab stitches (see page 19) are used to secure the felt to the fabric; these should be very neat and as small as possible.

Take your time when stuffing the shapes; a smoother finish will be achieved by slowly building up the shape with small amounts of stuffing.

1 Stab stitch round the shape; bring the needle out of the fabric at an angle, then take it down through the edge of the felt. Leave a small gap.

2 Use a cocktail stick to push stuffing into the pouch. When you have achieved the required shape, close the gap with more stab stitches.

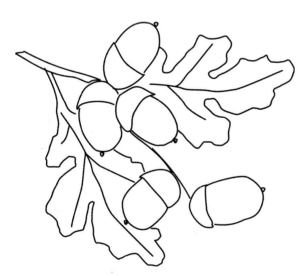

Full-size pattern. Use gold fabric paint or gel pen to transfer all the outlines on to the background fabric.

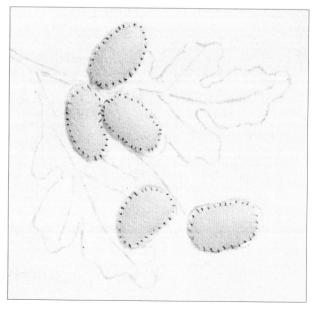

All padding stuffed and sewn on to the background fabric.

Working the acorns

Start the embroidery by using stem stitch and satin stitch to embroider the stalks and leaves respectively. Then, using a No. 7 embroidery needle and one strand of six-stranded cotton, cover the whole of each padded acorn shape with long satin stitches. Start in the middle of a shape, work across to one side, then go back and work the other side. Finish each acorn with a small French knot at the top. Now use the same needle and thread and Ceylon stitch to create the texture of the acorn cups as shown below.

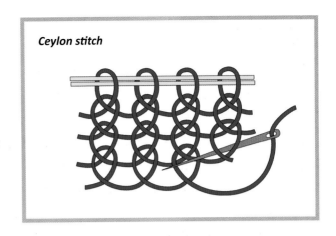

Ceylon stitch

1 Form the top edge of the cup with two satin stitches across the acorn, about halfway down the shape.

2 Bring the thread up at one side of the acorn, then work a row of slightly spaced buttonhole stitches, see page 24, over the two satin stitches.

3 Take the thread down behind the acorn shape, bring it back up on the other side slightly below the last row, then work a row of Ceylon stitches through the loops in the first row.

4 Repeat step 3 until the cup is complete.

The finished embroidery.

Poppy Seed Heads

Although these poppy seed heads are quite round in appearance, they are not as smooth as the acorns in the previous project. Felt is still used as the padding material but, here, three layers of felt are sewn on top of each other.

The bulk of each seed head shape is covered with satin stitch (see page 21) and rows of stem stitch (see page 20) create the stalks. The textured top to each seed head is worked on a shaped piece of thin suede and consists of bullion knots worked from the tip of the seed head down to the points of the shape.

Materials

Embroidery hoop
Medium-weight calico
Scissors
Felt for padding
Thin suede
Tracing paper and pencil
Fabric paint and brush
Sewing thread
Six-stranded cotton
No. 7 embroidery needle

Full-size pattern. Use gold fabric paint or gel pen to transfer all the outlines of this pattern on to the background fabric.

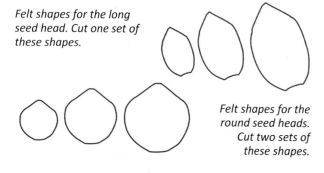

Felt shapes for the long seed head. Cut one set of these shapes.

Felt shapes for the round seed heads. Cut two sets of these shapes.

Layering the felt padding

Layering felt is an ideal method of padding the shapes of these seed heads. Referring to the small diagram (below left), cut out sets of three different-sized shapes for each seed head.

Then, starting with the smallest shape, use small, neat stab stitches (see page 19) to secure them on top of each other within the gold outlines on the background fabric.

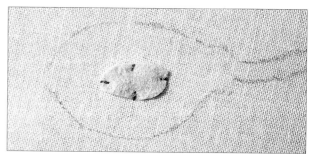

1 Use just four stab stitches to secure the smallest shape in the middle of the outline.

2 Overlay the second layer, secure it initially with four stitches, then stab stitch it all round.

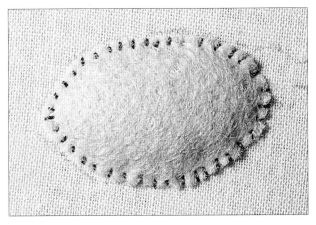

3 Stab stitch the third layer to complete the padding.

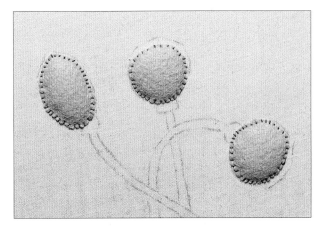

4 Work the other two seed head shapes in a similar manner.

 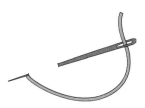

Embroidering the design

Use a No. 7 embroidery needle and one strand of six-stranded cotton to work the stalks on the background fabric; make four or five rows of stem stitch, side by side.

Use long satin stitches to cover the seed heads, working from the top to the bottom of each shape. Work satin stitch across the join between the stalk and the seed head.

Draw the shapes for the tops of the seed heads on to a piece of thin suede. Work six bullion knots on each shape; start each stitch at the top centre of the shape and take it down to one of the points. Trim the shapes to size, then sew them over the top of the seed heads, leaving the bottom of each shape free.

The finished embroidery.

Topiary

In this project, only the short lengths of tree trunk, worked in stem stitch (see page 20), are embroidered on the background fabric. The circles of foliage are slips, worked entirely in French knots on a separate piece of lightweight calico. These slips need little or no filling, as the surplus calico provides the stuffing. However, a more rounded effect can be achieved by adding toy stuffing.

Petite beads, to represent berries, are sewn on the completed mass of French knot foliage. Air-drying clay is used to make the flowerpot, but you can also buy flowerpot buttons.

Materials

- Embroidery hoop
- Medium-weight calico
- Scissors
- Lightweight calico
- Tracing paper and pencil
- Fabric paint and brush
- Sewing thread
- Six-stranded cotton
- No. 7 embroidery needle
- No.10 sharps or a beading needle
- Petite beads
- Air-drying clay
- Pin
- Acrylic paint

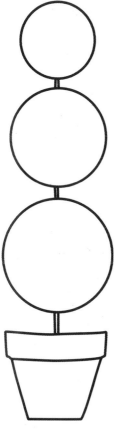

Full-size pattern. Use gold fabric paint or gel pen to transfer all the outlines of this pattern on to the background fabric.

Making French knot slips

Paint the three circles on a separate piece of lightweight calico, leaving at least 25mm (1in) space between each for cutting out, then fill each circle with a mass of French knots.

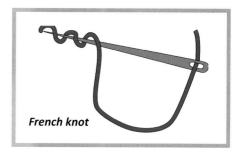

French knot

1 Bring the thread up through the fabric, hold the thread taut, then twist the needle round the thread twice.

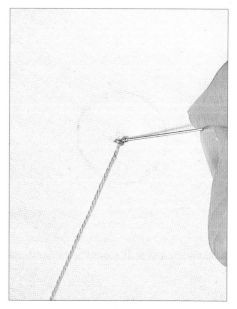

2 Keeping the thread taut, take the needle back through the fabric just to the side of where the thread comes through it.

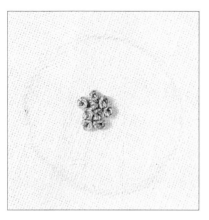

3 Release the thread when the needle has gone through the fabric. Pull the knot tight, then repeat.

4 When the shape is full, work small running stitches approximately 6mm (¼in) away from the embroidery. Leave a tail of thread at one end.

5 Cut out the shape, 6mm (¼in) outside the running stitches, then pull the thread to draw the surplus calico up behind the embroidery.

6 Flatten the shape, tucking in the surplus fabric, then secure the loose thread with a couple of stitches. Make the other two slips in the same way.

7 Roll out the clay, cut it into the flowerpot shape, then add a lip along the top edge. Use a pin to make two small holes in the middle of the pot. When the pot is dry, paint it with acrylics and leave it to dry again.

8 Use stab stitches (see page 19) to secure the slips over the painted shapes on the background fabric. Then, using a beading needle and a complementary colour of thread, randomly sew on the fine beads between the French knots.

The finished embroidery. Before sewing the three decorated slips to the background fabric, work the short lengths of the trunk in stem stitch (see page 20). Finally, when the paint is thoroughly dry, sew the flowerpot to the embroidery.

Butterfly

The three-dimensional effects of this butterfly design are all achieved with embroidery stitches; no extra padding is used. The outline of the butterfly is worked in stem stitch (see page 20). Satin stitch, overlaid with raised stem stitch band, creates the body parts. The other decoration is worked with satin stitch (see page 21), padded satin stitch (see page 35), spider's web stitch (see page 34) and a few French knots (see page 30). The coloured diagram below shows where these different stitches are used.

Full-size pattern. Use gold fabric paint or gel pen to mark all the outlines on to the background fabric.

Stem stitch

Use stem stitch (see page 20) to work the outlines of the wings, the two half circles in the lower wings, the two small circles at the bottom of the wings and all the straight lines.

Satin stitch with French knot at the end

Stem stitch

Satin stitch

Padded satin stitch

French knots

Spider's web stitch

Raised stem stitch band

This stitch makes a solid, raised filling that can only be worked in straight rows, from either the top to the bottom or the bottom to the top. It can be worked in a single colour or as rows of different colours. The length of stem stitch can be varied by increasing or decreasing the distance between the straight stitch bars.

Raised stem stitch band

Work the two parts of the body separately, within each outlined shape. Use complementary colours for the satin stitch base and the straight stitch bars. For clarity, different colours have been used in the diagrams below.

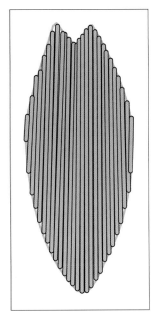

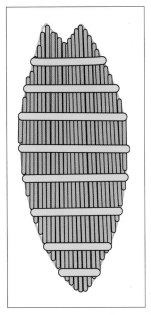

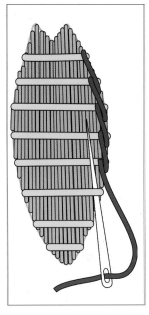

1 Using all six strands of cotton, fill each shape with satin stitches. If you want a more rounded body, sew more layers over the centre section.

2 Next, using one strand of six-stranded cotton, sew a series of spaced straight stitch bars across the body.

3 Finally, work stem stitches over the short straight stitches, making sure you do not pick up the stitches underneath.

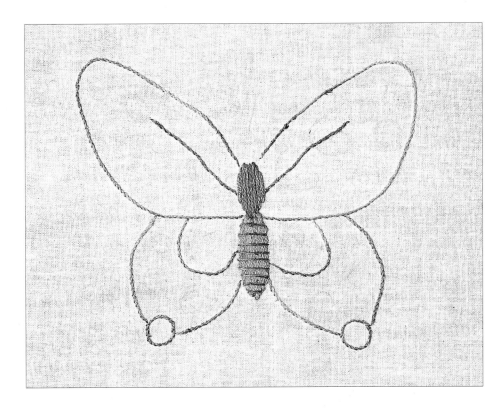

In this photograph, the two halves of the body are at different stages. The top part is complete, while the lower part is ready for the final stem stitches to be applied.

33

Spider's web stitch

This stitch is used to embroider the three small circles in each of the lower wings. Contrasting colours have been used in the following diagrams so that the stitches can be seen clearly. For the actual project, use one strand of six-stranded cotton in the same colour or complementary colours.

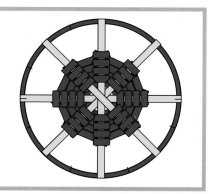

Spider's web stitch
Spider's web stitch is worked on ribs of threads laid across a back-stitched outline round the area to be embroidered (see page 52).

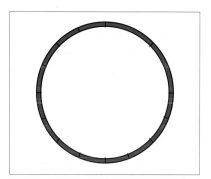

1 Referring to the coloured diagram on page 32, back stitch (see page 52) round the outlines of the shapes to be worked with spider's web stitch.

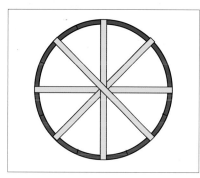

2 Now, bring the thread up at the edge of the shape, take it across the middle, then down through the opposite edge. Take the thread across the underside of the fabric and bring it back up to the front where you want the next rib to start. Make three more ribs in a similar manner.

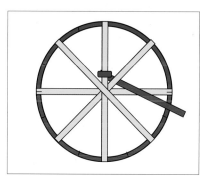

3 When all the ribs have been made, bring the thread up through the centre of the circle, just to the side of one of the ribs. Take the thread back over and under that rib, then under the next rib. Note that the thread does not pass through the fabric.

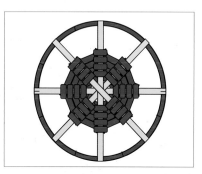

4 Take the thread back over and under this rib, then under the next. Continue working round the circle, taking the thread back over one rib then under two, until the desired portion of the circle has been filled. Fasten the thread on the underside of the fabric.

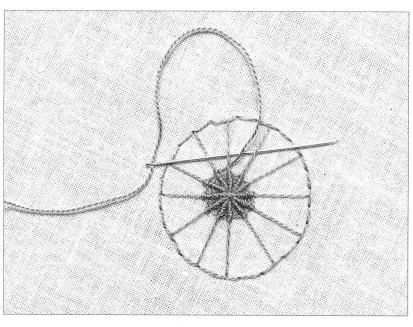

Enlarged view of spider's web stitch in progress.

34

Padded satin stitch

The three circles on each of the upper wings and the butterfly's head are worked with three layers of satin stitch. Each layer is sewn in a different direction on progressively larger circles. Again, for clarity, different colours are used on the diagrams for each layer. For the actual embroidery, use the same or a complementary colour of thread for each layer.

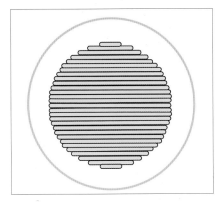 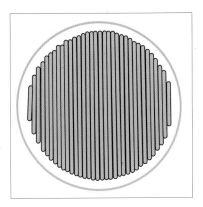 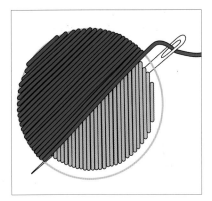

1 First, working an area 3mm (⅛in) inside the drawn circle, fill it with a layer of closely worked satin stitches (see page 21).

2 Now, working an area 1.5mm (¹⁄₁₆in) inside the drawn circle, sew a second layer of closely worked satin stitches at right angles to the first.

3 Finally, work a third layer of satin stitches at an angle of about 45-degrees to the previous layer to cover the whole of the drawn area.

Other stitches

The lozenge shapes on the upper wing are worked in satin stitch (see page 21). The antennae are single, long straight stitches with tiny French knots (see page 30) on the end. More French knots and straight stitches complete the design on the lower wings.

The photograph of the finished embroidery, right, clearly shows the detail on the body and wings: note the padded satin stitch circles and the satin stitch lozenges on the upper wings. Note how interest has been created by varying the direction of the final layer of stitches on each of the circles.

Needlelace techniques

Needlelace is a technique that is well worth incorporating into stumpwork as it provides lots of textures that cannot be obtained with other embroidery stitches.

Small fragments of lace can be applied to the background fabric or over padded shapes. They can be stiffened with horsehair, to make them stand proud of the surface, or with fine wire to allow them to be bent into freestanding shapes.

Needlelace is worked over a cordonnet (a strong cotton thread laid round the shape to be filled), which is temporarily couched on a needlelace pad with sewing thread. The needlelace pad consists of two or three layers of a backing material, a paper pattern and an overlay to protect the paper pattern from the needle. The filling stitches, which are all variations of detached buttonhole stitch, are all worked with 100/3 silk thread.

In this part of the book, we show you the basic principles of making a simple outline cordonnet (a leaf shape with a centre vein) and how to fill it with two types of filling stitch. We then take you, step by step, through the projects on this sampler, before moving on to more complex designs.

Leaf

Most needlelace shapes have simple outlines, where the cordonnet threads are joined on one side of the shape (see page 44). However, some shapes, such as this leaf with a centre vein, need careful planning to ensure they are able to support the finished needlelace. On these pages you will learn how to make a needlelace pad and how to plan the cordonnet for the leaf. You will also learn two basic filling stitches.

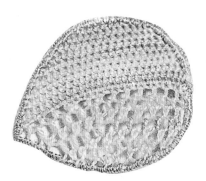

Finished leaf.

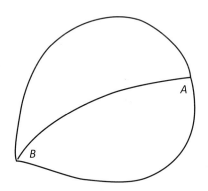

Full-size pattern for the leaf shape.

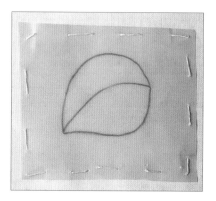

Leaf needlelace pad.

Needlelace pad

You can make small needlelace pads to suit individual shapes or make them large enough to accommodate several pieces. If you use the latter method, it is best to complete all the shapes on the pad before releasing any of them. Make a sandwich of two or three layers of medium-weight calico, the paper pattern and a transparent, protective overlay.

We use architect's linen to protect the paper patterns, but self-adhesive plastic film, which is more readily available, is just as good. Tack all the layers together firmly.

Making a cordonnet

It is essential that cordonnets stay intact when the needlelace is released from the backing fabric, so joins must be kept to a minimum. Take time to plan the layout properly so that you can build a cordonnet from a continuous length of crochet thread. Use the full-size pattern to estimate the length of thread required. Lay the thread along all the lines on the diagram including the central vein, double this length and add a short extra allowance. You will need 380mm (15in) of thread for this leaf.

The steps on the following page show you how to build this particular shape, with its intersections at each end of the centre vein. A more complicated leaf shape, with lots of intersecting veins, is shown on page 104, but it is just an extension of these basic rules.

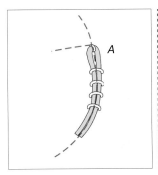

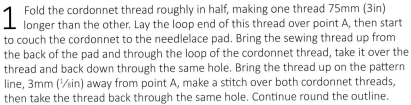
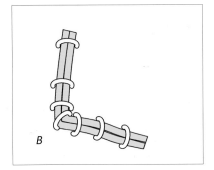

1 Fold the cordonnet thread roughly in half, making one thread 75mm (3in) longer than the other. Lay the loop end of this thread over point A, then start to couch the cordonnet to the needlelace pad. Bring the sewing thread up from the back of the pad and through the loop of the cordonnet thread, take it over the thread and back down through the same hole. Bring the thread up on the pattern line, 3mm (1/8in) away from point A, make a stitch over both cordonnet threads, then take the thread back through the same hole. Continue round the outline.

2 When you reach point B, make an extra couching stitch at the point of the leaf (a sharp point is useful when making the filling stitches). Continue couching round the outer edge of the leaf back towards point A.

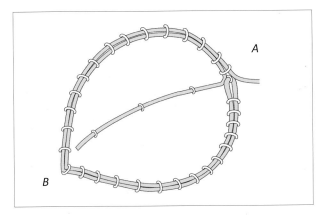

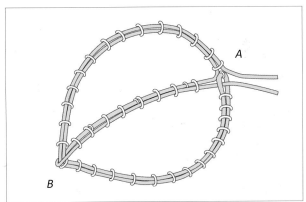

3 When you get back to point A, separate the cordonnet threads. Take the long one towards point B, couching it down in two or three places to hold it in position.

4 At point B, take the thread under and over the couched outline threads, lay it back down against the single thread, pass it through the original loop at point A, then couch down both threads to complete the vein.

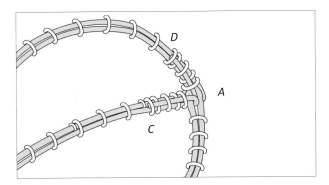

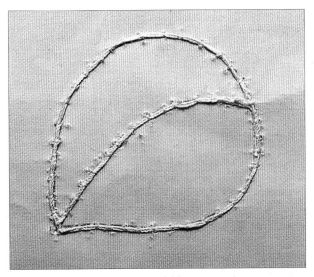

5 At point A, fold the thread back on itself, then couch down a short length to point C. Use a large-eyed needle to pull the other thread through the original loop, fold it back to point D, then couch it down. Fasten off the couching thread on the back of the pad, then trim excess threads.

The finished cordonnet.

Filling stitches

One half of the leaf design is filled with single Brussels stitch, the other with corded single Brussels stitch. Both halves are worked from the central vein out to the edges. The filling stitches do not pass through the sandwiched layers of the needlelace pad, but are worked over and supported on the cordonnet threads.

Joins in the filling stitches can only be made at the end of each row, so you must ensure that you always have sufficient thread to work a full row of stitches. A good guide is to have at least three to four times the length of the space being worked.

To help maintain an even tension, and therefore keep your stitches neat, it is advisable to work on a needlelace pillow (see below). Pin your needlelace pad securely on the pillow with berry pins.

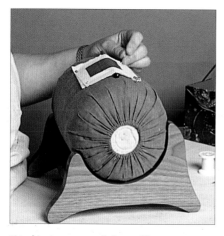

Working on a needlelace pillow.

Single Brussels stitch

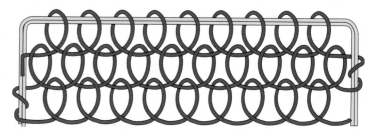

Start this stitch with a row of buttonhole stitches, see page 24, across the cordonnet. The spacing of this foundation row of stitches governs the texture of the finished piece: use loose stitches for an open texture; tight ones for a dense texture. Subsequent rows of stitches are looped into those above.

Corded single Brussels stitch

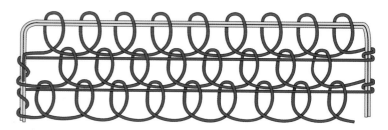

This stitch is worked in much the same way as that above except that, at the end of each row of buttonhole stitches, the thread is laid back across the work as a 'cord', then the next row of stitches is worked round this cord and the loops in the previous row.

Both of these examples have the same number of stitches in the row, but notice how the corded version has a denser structure.

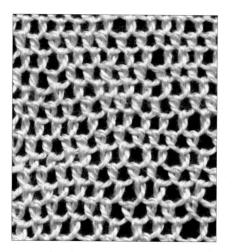

Single Brussels stitch.

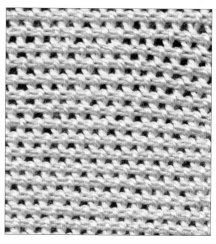

Corded single Brussels stitch.

40

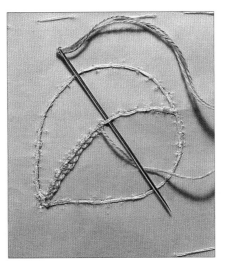

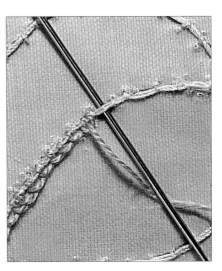

1 Secure the end of the 100/3 silk thread to the cordonnet by passing it under a few of the couching stitches. Take it through to a point just short of the intersection between the centre vein and the outline of the leaf.

2 Work a row of evenly spaced buttonhole stitches across the central vein of the cordonnet. Do not pull the stitches too tight as you must work through their loops for the next row.

This enlarged view of the first row of buttonhole stitches shows how the loops are formed as you progress.

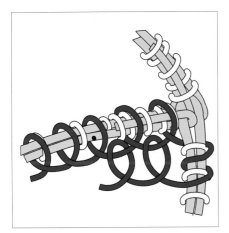

3 When you reach the end of the row attach the thread to the side of the cordonnet. Take the needle and thread under both cordonnet threads, then whip it over *both* threads – allowing for the depth of the stitches – down to the point where you want to start the next row.

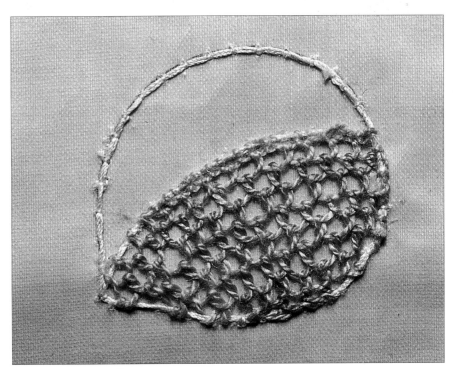

4 Work back across the shape, working one buttonhole stitch in each loop of the previous row. Whip the thread round the cordonnet again then work back across the shape. Continue until the area is filled. Always take your needle and thread straight out under the cordonnet threads – this will help to keep the rows straight. Secure the last row of stitches by whipping each loop to the cordonnet.

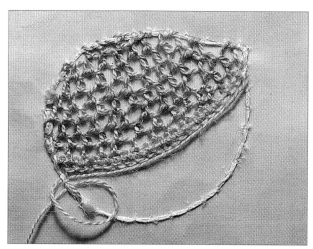

5 Turn the leaf shape round, attach another silk thread to the cordonnet, then work a row of buttonhole stitches, slightly tighter than those in step 2, across the centre vein. At the end of the row, take the thread under, over and under the cordonnet.

6 Lay the thread back across the space, just under the loops of the first row, to form the cord. At the left-hand edge of the design whip the thread down the cordonnet to the start point for the next row of stitches.

7 Work another row of buttonhole stitches; this time, work the stitches into each loop of the previous row and under the laid cord.

8 Repeat steps 6 and 7 until the whole area is filled, then whip the last row of loops to the cordonnet as in step 4.

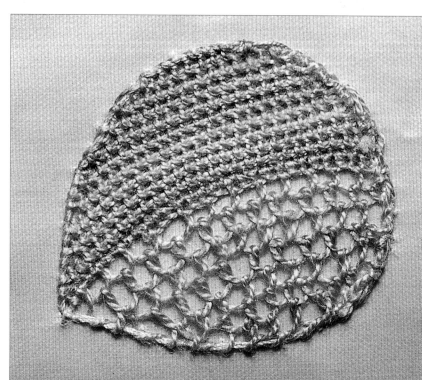

Top stitching and releasing the needlelace

One characteristic of needlelace is a raised outer edge. This is made by laying two threads over the cordonnet, then covering these and the cordonnet threads with a row of buttonhole stitches. Work the buttonhole stitches as close together as possible, preferably with the loops lying towards the outer edge of the shape. When the top stitching is complete, the needlelace is released from the fabric backing and assembled on the embroidery.

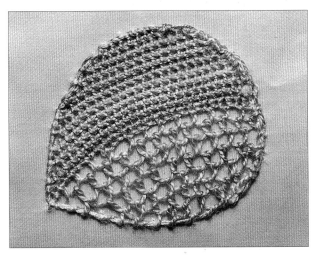

1 Cut another length of cordonnet thread long enough to go twice around the shape, with a little extra for good measure (see page 38). Fold it in half, then use the silk thread to whip the loop end to the existing cordonnet threads. Now, using the silk thread, work tight buttonhole stitches all round the shape.

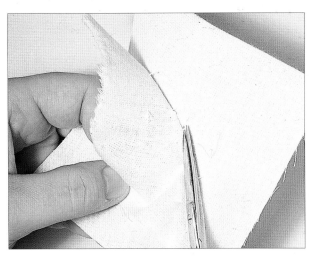

2 Remove the tacking stitches around the design, fold back the bottom layer of calico, then use fine-pointed scissors to snip through all the couching stitches.

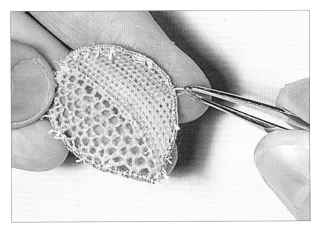

3 Remove the needlelace, then use a pair of tweezers to remove any remaining fragments of the couching threads from the back of the lace.

The completed leaf.

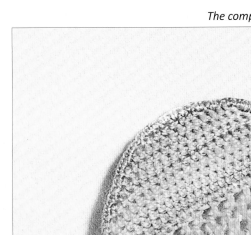

Flower

This first needlelace project is a simple flower design. The flower bud is raised on padded felt (see page 26). The stalks are paper-covered wire, which is wrapped with silk thread then couched on to the background fabric. The needlelace shapes are filled with single and corded single Brussels stitch (see page 40), and double Brussels stitch (see page 45). The freestanding petals are only secured at the centre of the flower. The base is a calico slip, covered with French knots.

Materials

- Needlelace pads (see page 38)
- Scissors
- Crochet thread No. 80
- Sewing thread
- Lightweight calico for the slip and finished embroidery
- Embroidery hoop
- Fabric paint and brushes
- No. 9 sharps needle
- Two No. 10 ballpoint needles
- 100/3 silk thread
- Felt for padding
- Toy stuffing
- Paper-covered wire
- PVA glue
- Fine knitting needle

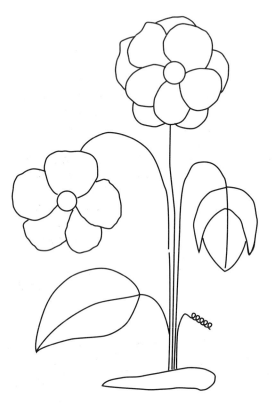

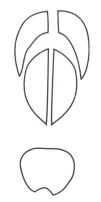

Cordonnet diagrams for petals and the parts of the bud.

Cordonnets

Referring to page 38, make needlelace pads for all the needlelace shapes. Use the exploded diagrams, left, for all the petals and the bud, and the full-size pattern, far left, for the leaf shape (please note that this is not exactly the same shape as the leaf shape on page 38).

Transfer the shape of the base on to a piece of lightweight calico in preparation for a slip.

Full-size pattern. The flower petals are freestanding, so use gold fabric paint or gel pen to transfer just the three long stalks, the leaf and its stalk, the bud shape and the centres of the two flowers on to the base fabric.

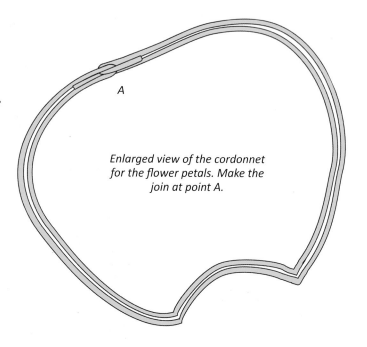

A

Enlarged view of the cordonnet for the flower petals. Make the join at point A.

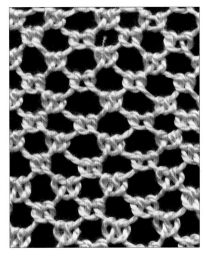

This is similar to single Brussels stitch, except that the first row of buttonhole stitches consists of spaced pairs of stitches – the space between each pair being the width of a pair of stitches. On subsequent rows, pairs of stitches are worked over the loops between the pairs of stitches in the row above.

Double Brussels stitch.

Needlelace petals

Referring to the general instructions on page 38 and the cordonnet diagram, build cordonnets for each petal. Start at point A, take the doubled crochet thread round the shape, pass both threads through the loop, turn them back and couch down the ends.

Make five petal shapes filled with single Brussels stitch (see page 40) and ten more filled with double Brussels stitch (see above). Top stitch round the outside of each petal as detailed on page 43.

Needlelace bud

The cordonnets for the bud parts are laid in a similar way to the petals, then each shape is filled with corded single Brussels stitch (see page 40). Do not top stitch round these shapes.

Needlelace leaf

For this project, the leaf includes a turned-over section which is worked over the top of the basic leaf shape before top stitching it. When filling curved shapes with corded needlelace, you will have more control over the cord by working with two needles.

Make a cordonnet for the leaf similar to that on page 39, then fill one half with single Brussels stitch and the other with corded single Brussels stitch (see page 40). Do not top stitch the shape yet. Work the turned-over shape with two needles and two lengths of thread as described below – for clarity, the two threads are shown in different colours.

Attach the first thread (shown in green) to the centre vein of the cordonnet, then make a row of buttonhole stitches along the outer edge of the leaf, over the previously worked needlelace. Whip the thread round the right-hand end of the cordonnet, then lay the thread back across the shape and take it under the left-hand end of the cordonnet. Do not secure this thread.

Attach the other thread (shown in pink) to the cordonnet, then start to work a second row of buttonhole stitches into the loops of the previous row and over the loose-laid cord.

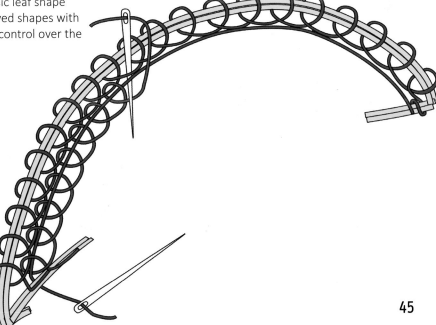

Working a curved shape using two needles.

45

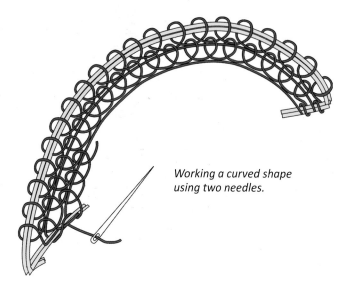

Working a curved shape using two needles.

When you reach the end of the second row, whip the thread round the left-hand end of the cordonnet, then lay the thread back across the row and under the right-hand end of the cordonnet. Do not secure this thread. Pick up the first needle and thread, whip it round the cordonnet, then start to work the third row of stitches.

Finish the third row of stitches, whip the thread round the right-hand end, then lay the thread back. Make a fourth row of stitches with the other thread then, instead of laying a cord, whip the thread back across the shape, working into each loop of the last row of stitches. Fasten off both threads into the cordonnet. Top stitch round the outer edge of the whole leaf shape and along the centre vein, then release from the pad as shown on page 43. Do not top stitch round the loose edge of the turnover section.

Finishing the embroidery

When all the needlelace parts of the design have been made, the embroidery can be assembled.

1 Measure the lengths of the three flower stalks and the leaf stalk, then cut a length of paper-covered wire for each. Dip one end of a wire into PVA glue, then, starting 25mm (1in) from the tip, loosely wrap silk thread back towards the tip. At the tip, pinch the thread into the glue, then wrap the thread as closely as possible down the length of the wire. Secure the end of the thread with a touch more glue. Couch all four stalks over the outlines on the background fabric (see page 23).

2 Make the short twisted stalk by winding a wrapped stem around a fine knitting needle or a large bodkin needle. Couch this on to the background fabric.

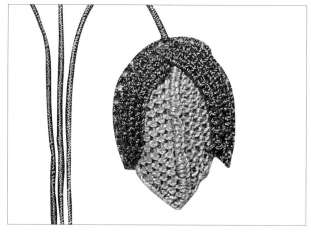

3 Referring to the full-size pattern on page 44, cut a piece of felt slightly smaller than the bud shape. Then, referring to page 26, sew this felt shape inside the gold outline on the background fabric and fill it with toy stuffing. Sew the needlelace bud pieces over the felt pad.

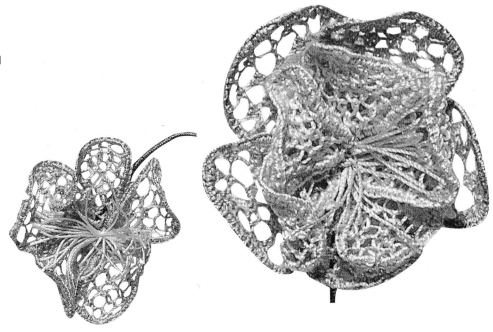

4 Sew the small sides of five of the double Brussels stitch petals round the gold outline of each flower centre. Overlap the petals slightly to make them look natural.

5 Sew the five single Brussels stitch petals over the double Brussels stitch petals on the top flower head.

6 Make the centres for the flowers. Cut a 20cm (8in) length of yellow silk thread. Thread one end of this into a needle, then wrap 15cm (6in) of the other end round a pencil. Carefully slip the wrapping from the pencil, catch the loops together with the needle and thread, then sew the loop securely in the middle of a flower head. Cut the loops and fray the ends out to resemble stamens.

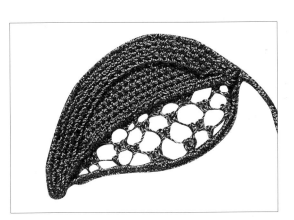

7 Sew the leaf over the end of its stalk.

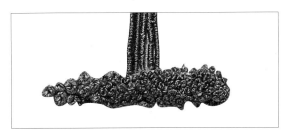

8 Use the base shape (see pattern on page 44) to make a small slip filled with French knots. Sew this over the bottom of the stalks.

The finished embroidery.

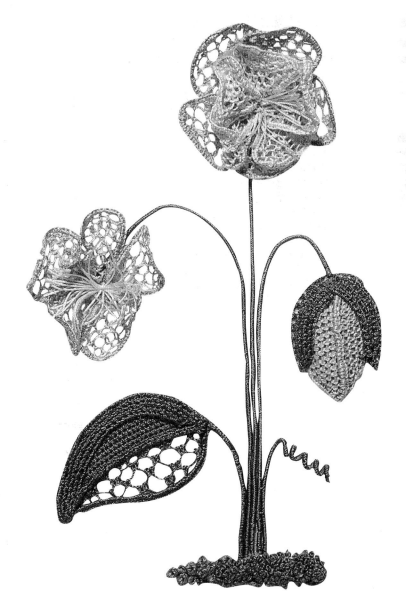

Seaweed and Fish

In this project, all the needlelace shapes are worked in corded single Brussels stitch (see page 40). The edges of the seaweed shapes are wired before they are top stitched to allow them to be entwined and stand free. The two striped fish, which are worked in two colours, are applied over layered felt (see page 28). The two rocks are slips made from painted lightweight calico stretched over pieces of interfacing.

Materials
- Needlelace pads (see page 38)
- Scissors
- Crochet thread No. 80
- Sewing thread
- Lightweight calico for the slip and the finished embroidery
- Embroidery hoop
- Fabric paint and brushes
- No. 9 sharps needle
- No. 10 ballpoint needle
- 100/3 silk thread
- Felt for padding
- Petite bead
- Fine wire
- Interfacing (or card)
- Sequins

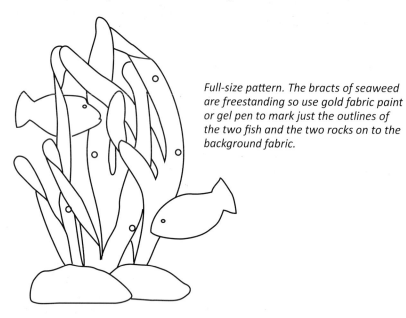

Full-size pattern. The bracts of seaweed are freestanding so use gold fabric paint or gel pen to mark just the outlines of the two fish and the two rocks on to the background fabric.

Cordonnets

Use the exploded diagram to make cordonnets for the four bracts of seaweed and the two fish. Remember to make the joins on one of the long edges of each shape.

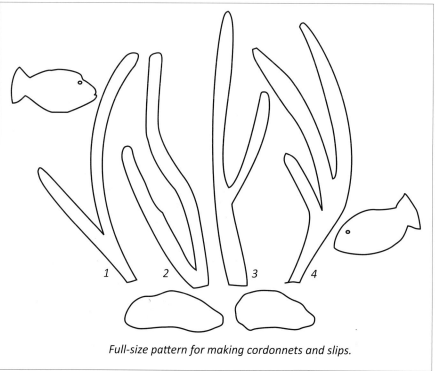

Full-size pattern for making cordonnets and slips.

Changing colours

This diagram shows corded single Brussels stitch, but the same method of
changing colour works with any filling stitch.

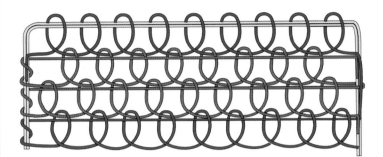 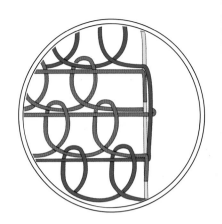

*Join the first colour thread to one side of the cordonnet, then work filling stitches down to the point
where you want to change colour. At the end of this row of buttonhole stitches, leave the thread to
one side (do not lay the thread back across the row).*

*Join the new colour to the cordonnet, lay it as a cord across the shape, whip it down the other side,
then work filling stitches in this colour until you want to change colour once more. If you intend
using the second colour again, leave it to one side. Otherwise, run it through the couching stitches
on the cordonnet and trim off the excess thread. Run the first colour thread down through the
couching stitches on the cordonnet to a point level with the bottom of the last row of stitches, lay in
a cord, then work filling stitches in the rest of the shape or until you want to change colour again.*

Needlelace fish

The two striped fish are worked with two needles
threaded with different colours as shown in the diagram
above. The petite bead used for the fish's eye is threaded
on to one of the laid cords, then the next row of filling
stitches is worked around the bead at the required
position. Alternatively, you could make the eye with
a small French knot. Do not top stitch round the fish
shapes, as they are applied to padded shapes on the
background fabric.

Needlelace seaweed

Fill all the shapes with corded single Brussels stitch.
Loosely whip a length of fine wire round each shape,
then top stitch and release each shape (see page 43).
Reinforcing the edges of these shapes with fine wire,
instead of the usual two threads, make the bracts stiffer
and easier to mould into shape.

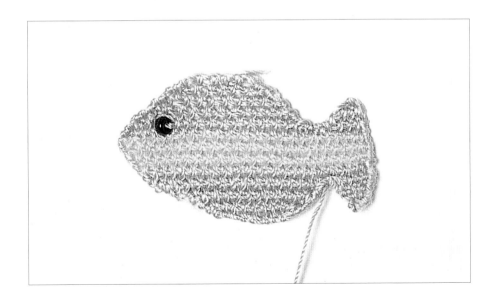

*Enlarged view of one of
the striped fish.*

Finishing the embroidery

1 Sew the bottom edges of the seaweed bracts on to the background fabric, overlapping them so that their fronds can be entwined. Most of the left-hand side of the long stem of seaweed shape 3 (see page 48) and the right-hand side of shape 4 are also sewn to the background fabric, leaving just their top ends free.

4 The rock shapes are slips of lightweight calico, painted with pearlised colour to give the rocks a textured appearance. The painted area of calico should be large enough to cut out oversize shapes with an allowance of 6mm (¼in) all round. When the paint is thoroughly dry, decorate the shape with embroidery detail (if required), then cut them out. Cut full-size rock shapes from a piece of interfacing (or cardboard if you want stiffer rocks). Stretch the calico over the interfacing shapes and lightly glue the turned-over edges to the back of the interfacing. Stab stitch the bottom edges of the rocks over the base of the seaweed.

2 Referring to the pattern on page 48 and the layered felt instructions on page 28, cut three layers of felt for each fish shape. Make the largest shape slightly smaller than the pattern, and omit the shape of the tails on all layers. Working from the smallest shape upwards, stab stitch each one to the background fabric, overlapping the sewn-down parts of the seaweed.

3 Stab stitch the needlelace fish shapes over the felt pads; secure just their bodies, leaving their tails free to give the impression that they are swimming. Sew a few sequins onto the seaweed, as directed by the pattern, to look like air bubbles.

The finished embroidery.

The inspiration for this picture came from a visit to a marine aquatic centre. The seahorse seemed to be motionless and oblivious to the hustle and bustle of the brightly coloured fish around him. The seahorse is worked in needlelace over a stuffed felt pad. The fish are calico-covered interfacing slips, embroidered with satin stitch. The seaweed is cut from two layers of painted silk bonded together with iron-on interfacing. The pattern for the seahorse is shown on page 166.

Orange Branch

This design includes five realistic oranges, which are made by covering cotton moulds with single Brussels stitch. The leaves are made in much the same way as those shown previously, using both single and double Brussels stitch. However, three of the leaves are worked on the background fabric of the finished embroidery, using a cordonnet of back stitches.

Materials
- Needlelace pads (see page 38)
- Scissors
- Crochet thread No. 80
- Sewing thread
- Lightweight calico for the finished embroidery
- Embroidery hoop
- Fabric paint and brushes
- Cotton moulds
- No. 9 sharps needle
- No. 10 ballpoint needle
- 100/3 silk thread
- Six-stranded cotton
- Fine wire
- Horsehair
- Stiletto
- Cocktail stick
- PVA glue

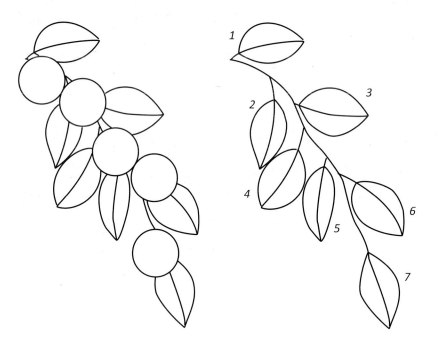

Full-size patterns for the design and the cordonnets for the leaf shapes. Use gold fabric paint or gel pen to transfer the outline of the branch, the leaf stalks and leaf shapes 1, 2 and 7 on to the background fabric.

Cordonnets

Use the full-size patterns to make cordonnets for leaf shapes 3, 4, 5 and 6, as described on pages 38–39. Work the cordonnets of leaf shapes 1, 2 and 7 on the background fabric by back stitching round the gold outline of each shape.

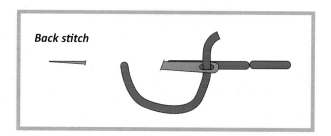

Back stitch

52

Needlelace oranges

The oranges are cotton moulds covered with needlelace. Unlike the other leaf shapes and the stalks, which are worked with silk thread, these are worked with one strand of six-stranded cotton.

It's a good idea to paint cotton moulds to match the colour of the thread used to cover them. This is not essential, but a painted mould does mask any irregularities in the needlelace. However, for clarity, a plain white cotton mould was used for these step-by-step photographs.

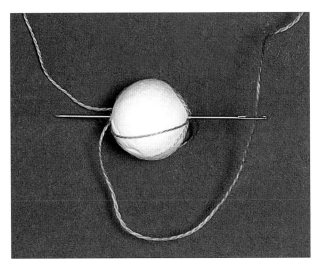

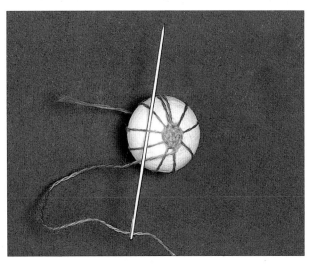

1 Using a No. 9 embroidery needle, take a long length of cotton thread down through the centre of the mould, bring the thread up round the outside of the mould, then back down through the centre to form a vertical stitch round the mould. Continue until you have made approximately ten evenly spaced stitches.

2 Cut a new length of cotton thread and bring the thread up through to the top of the cotton mould. Weave this thread through the vertical stitches, taking it round two or three times.

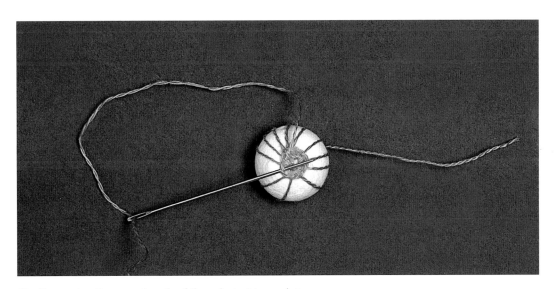

3 Now, using the same length of thread, start to work tiny single Brussels stitches, see page 40, as close together as possible, over the last row of woven threads. You can disregard the vertical stitches, which have now served their purpose.

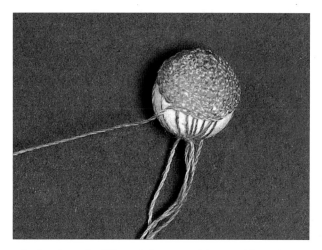

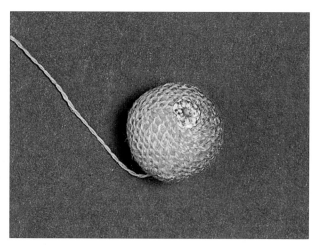

4 Continue the filling stitches round the mould, working them into the loops of the stitches immediately above. As the shape gets bigger, increase the number of stitches by working two loops into one. When the thread starts to run out, take the short end down, round the outside of the mould, to the bottom and anchor it under two or three of the vertical stitches. Attach a new length of thread under the same vertical stitches, bring it up to the needlelace and link it through the last completed loop, then continue working the filling stitches.

5 When you pass the widest part of the mould, decrease the stitches by missing out some of the loops in the previous row. When the whole mould is covered, trim off the excess lengths of all bar one of the loose threads. Use a cocktail stick to apply a spot of glue to the underside of the cotton mould, then push all the trimmed lengths into the recess. Finally, using one strand of green cotton thread, work a few rows of buttonhole stitches over the orange ones.

Needlelace leaves

Make leaf shapes 3, 4, 5 and 6 in needlelace, using your choice of filling stitches. Before top stitching them, lay one strand of horsehair round leaf shapes 4 and 6, and one strand of fine wire round leaf shapes 3 and 5. Leave tails of horsehair and fine wire at the base of each leaf shape to attach the shapes to the background fabric.

Fill leaf shapes 1, 2 and 7 with your choice of filling stitches, within the back-stitched cordonnets on the background fabric. Do not top stitch round these shapes.

Finishing the embroidery

Work the branch and the short leaf stalks in stem stitch. Decide on the arrangement of the freestanding leaves and oranges. Use a stiletto to make small holes in the background fabric at the appropriate places, take the wire and horsehair tails on the leaves, and the cotton thread on the oranges, through to the back of the work, then secure them with a few oversewn stitches. Finally, shape the freestanding leaves.

The finished embroidery.

This design is typical of seventeenth-century stumpwork in that the fruit and leaves are completely out of proportion to the size of the tree. It is made entirely of needlelace shapes, worked in much the same way as the previous project. Eight different types of filling stitch are used for the base.

Mushrooms

All the elements of this design are needlelace shapes except for the four small patches of grass at the base of each mushroom, which are slips filled with French knots. All the padding is stuffed felt. The pads for the mushroom stalks are prepared in exactly the same way as in previous projects (see page 26), but the pads for the mushroom caps are left open along their bottom edges. The layered structure of the mushrooms means that the needlelace elements must be layered, with some pads sewn on top of needlelace shapes. This project introduces a new filling stitch and crossbar stitch, and the tops of some of the mushrooms are decorated with buttonholed loops.

Materials
- Needlelace pads (see page 38)
- Scissors
- Crochet thread No. 80
- Fabric paint and brush
- Sewing thread
- Lightweight calico for the slips and finished embroidery
- Embroidery hoop
- No. 9 sharps needle
- No. 10 ballpoint needle
- 100/3 silk thread
- Felt for padding
- Toy stuffing
- Cocktail stick

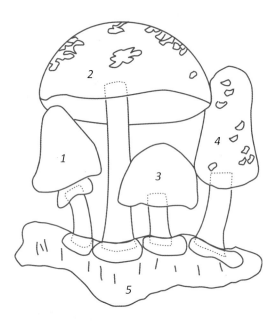

Full-size pattern. Use gold fabric paint or gel pen to outline the shapes of the mushroom heads, their stalks and the large grass base on to the background fabric. The dotted lines at the top and bottom of the stalks show the size of the shapes for the felt pads.

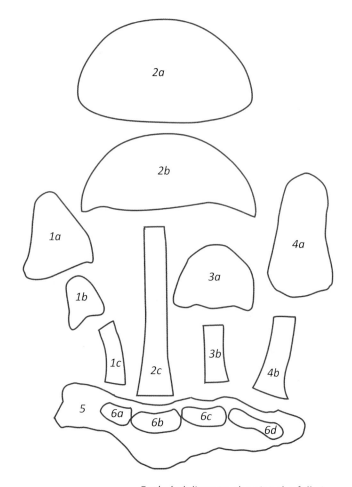

Exploded diagram showing the full-size shapes for the cordonnets and slips.

56

Cordonnets

Use the exploded diagram to make cordonnets for all shapes, except shapes 6a–6d, which are slips.

Slips

Prepare French knot slips for the four grass shapes 6a–6d (see pages 30–31).

Crossbar stitch

This is a variation of double Brussels stitch (see page 45). Make a foundation row of spaced pairs of stitches – the space between each pair being the width of a pair of stitches – then make a second row of stitches, looping

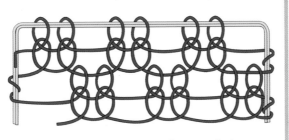

each stitch into the stitch above. On the next row, make two stitches into the loops between the pairs of stitches in the previous row, then make another row of stitches, looping each stitch into the stitch above. Repeat until the shape is filled.

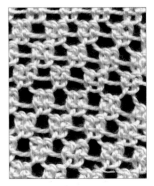

Enlarged view of crossbar stitch.

Needlelace shapes

Work the stalk shapes 1c, 2c, 3b and 4b, the mushroom cap shapes 1b, 2a, 2b and 4a, and the grass base shape 5 in corded single Brussels stitch.

Work the mushroom cap shape 1a in corded double Brussels stitch. Work the mushroom cap shape 3a in crossbar stitch.

Top stitch along just the bottom sections of cap shapes 1a, 1b, 2b, 3a and 4a. The cap shape 2a, the stalk shapes 1c, 2c, 3b and 4b, and the grass shape 5 do not require top stitching as they are sewn on to the background fabric.

Enlarged view of the needlelace shape 1a, which is worked in corded double Brussels stitch, and shape 3a, which is worked in crossbar stitch. Notice that base shapes are top stitched across the bottom edges.

Finishing the embroidery

1 Sew the needlelace grass shape 5 to the background fabric.

2 Referring to the full-size pattern on page 56, cut slightly undersize pieces of felt for the stalk shapes of all four mushrooms.

3 Stab stitch the felt shapes for mushrooms 1, 3 and 4 to the grass base and the background fabric, then fill them with toy stuffing using a cocktail stick (see page 26).

4 Apply the needlelace stalk shapes 1c, 3b and 4b over the felt pads.

5 Apply the ring shape 1b over its stalk. Sew just the sides and top to the background fabric, leaving the bottom edge free.

6 Cut a slightly undersize piece of felt for the cap of mushroom 4, then secure its sides and top edges to the background fabric. Fill the shape with toy stuffing, then, as the bottom of the felt shape is left open, secure the stuffing with three or four loose stab stitches approximately 6mm (¼in) up from the bottom of the felt. Take these stab stitches through to the back of the background fabric, but do not pull them tight. Apply the needlelace shape 4a over its felt pad, leaving the bottom edge free.

7 Sew the needlelace cap shape 2a to the background fabric and over the edge of mushroom cap shape 4a.

8 Stab stitch the felt stalk shape for mushroom 2 to the background fabric and over the bottom needlelace section of its cap, then fill it with toy stuffing. Sew the needlelace stalk shape 2c to its pad.

9 Referring to step 6, cut, apply and fill a piece of felt for the top section of the cap of mushroom 2, then apply the needlelace shape 2b over the felt pad. Remember to leave its bottom edge free.

10 Cut and apply a piece of felt for the cap of mushroom 1, laying a small section of this over the bottom part of the cap of mushroom 2. Fill the felt with toy stuffing, then apply the needlelace shape 1a over the felt pad.

11 Repeat step 10 for the cap of mushroom 3: a small part of this fits over the stalk of mushroom 2.

12 Referring to the diagram and instructions above, decorate the caps of mushrooms 2 and 4 by overstitching them with groups of five or seven buttonholed loops, sewn through all layers (see right).

13 Apply the four French knot slips over the bottom of the mushroom stalks, sewing them along just the bottom edges.

14 Finally, make some small tufts of grass in the same way as the stamens for the flower heads on page 47, then sew these to the grass base.

Buttonholed loops

Knot a silk thread, bring the needle up at point A, then back down through the work at point B – approximately 5mm (¼in) away – leaving a small loop. Repeat this stitch to make a three-stranded loop on the surface. Bring the thread back up at point A, then make a series of close buttonhole stitches over the loop. At the end of the loop, take the thread to the back of the work just above point B. Gently pull the thread to make the stitched loop twist up off the surface, then fasten off.

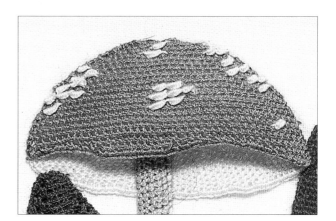

The finished embroidery.

Foxgloves

This design, with its tubular, bell-shaped flowers, introduces the use of a wooden embroidery shoe to make the needlelace shapes for the flower heads. Six of the flower heads are worked on normal needlelace pads, four are worked straight on cordonnets back stitched on the background fabric. All the needlelace pieces are filled with corded single Brussels stitch, then decorated with groups of French knots. The flower stalk is a slip of silk fabric stretched over a single layer of felt.

Materials

- Needlelace pads (see page 38)
- Scissors
- Crochet thread No. 80
- Sewing thread
- Lightweight calico for the finished embroidery
- Embroidery hoop
- Fabric paint and brushes
- No. 9 sharps needle
- No. 10 ballpoint needle
- 100/3 silk thread
- Wooden embroidery shoe
- Silk fabric
- Felt for padding
- Toy stuffing
- Cocktail stick
- PVA glue

Cordonnet diagrams for the caps and flower heads.

Full-size pattern. Use gold fabric paint or gel pen to outline the flower stalk and flower head shapes 1–4 on to the background fabric.

Cordonnets

Use the small diagrams above to prepare cordonnets for the flower heads and caps. Six of the flowers are worked on needlelace pads; four are worked on the background fabric. You only need to make eight caps, as the tops of flowers 1 and 2 are completely covered by other parts of the embroidery.

Each flower head consists of two layers of needlelace, so it is essential that the couching stitches used for the cordonnets that are made on needlelace pads are firm and close together. Use short back stitches to make the cordonnets for the flower heads 1–4 on the background fabric.

Needlelace flowers

Foxgloves are tubular in shape, and two layers of needlelace must be worked on the same cordonnet to make the shape. A wooden embroidery shoe keeps the top and bottom layers separate and helps to create a more rounded shape. Corded single Brussels stitch (see page 40) is used to fill both layers, but a slight variation is introduced on the last rows of the top piece to create a flared edge.

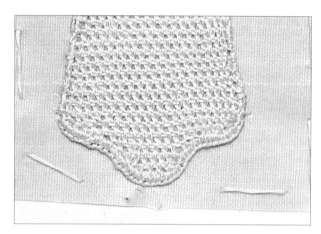

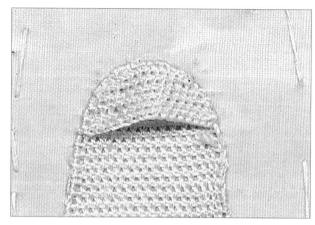

1 Make the bottom half of the eight loose flower heads on needlelace pads, filling the shape with corded single Brussels stitch.

2 Go back to the top of the cordonnet, then work five rows of corded single Brussels stitch over the bottom layer of needlelace.

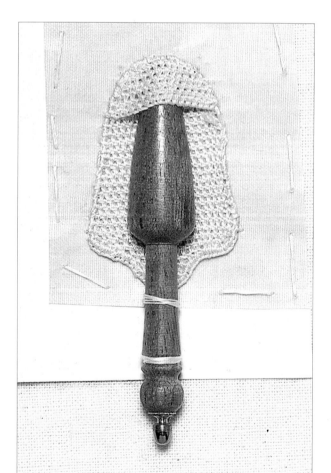

3 Place the wooden embroidery shoe under the five rows of the top layer and secure it in position with three or four oversewing stitches on the neck of the shoe.

4 Continue down the shape, working rows of stitches over the shoe until you are ready to finish the shape. Refer to the full-size pattern to determine the depth of each top layer.

5 At the end of a row of stitches, do not lay a cord across the shape. Instead, work back across the row making two stitches into the first loop of the previous row, one stitch into the next loop, two stitches into the next loop, etc.

6 Repeat step 5, lay a cord across the shape, top stitch over the cord and through each loop of the last row of filling stitches, then remove the flower and shoe from the backing pad.

7 Dab a few spots of PVA glue on a small amount of toy stuffing, then use a cocktail stick to push the stuffing up between the two layers of needlelace to create a tubular shape.

8 Referring to the image of the finished embroidery, right, decorate the flower head with a random group of French knots sewn into the bottom layer of needlelace.

9 Repeat steps 1–8 for the flower head shapes 1, 2, 3 and 4, over the back-stitched cordonnets on the background fabric.

Needlelace caps

Work eight caps for the foxgloves (flower head shapes 1 and 2 do not require these), top stitch all round each shape, then remove them from the backing pad.

Slip

Referring to the full-size pattern, cut a piece of felt to fit the shape of the stalk. Cut a piece of silk fabric, allowing for a 6mm (¼in) turnover on each edge. Secure the turnovers to the back of the felt with a few spots of PVA.

Finishing the embroidery

1 Sew the flower stalk slip to the background fabric, laying it over flower head shapes 1–4.

2 Sew the top ends of flower head shapes 5–10 to the stalk and background fabric.

3 Finally, sew the needlelace caps to the top of the flower heads, leaving the bottom edges free.

The finished embroidery.

Creating a scene

Here, you will learn to use embroidery, needlelace and other techniques to create an embroidered scene.

Birds and Beach

This delightful beach scene was inspired by some sketches made on holiday. The painted background adds a touch of realism to this type of embroidery. All the needlelace shapes are filled with single and corded single Brussels stitches. Satin stitch is used to cover some of the rocks and to define the birds' legs and beaks, and French knots form the birds' eyes. A new technique is also introduced – ruching tubular ribbon over lengths of double knitting wool – to create the waves.

Enlarge this diagram by 150% to make a full-size pattern. When the background washes have been fixed, use gold fabric paint or gel pen to outline the birds shapes B1–B4, all the rocks and the two posts on to the background fabric.

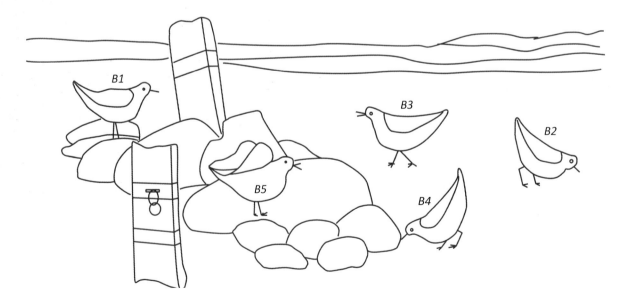

Painting the background

Dampen the top half of the background fabric with clean water, then lay in a wash of pale blue for the sky. Dampen the bottom half of the background fabric, leaving a small dry gap under the sky colour, then apply a wash of golden sand colour. Leave the fabric to dry completely, then iron it to set the paint. Use gold fabric paint or gel pen to outline the shapes for birds B1–B4, the rocks and the two posts on the background fabric.

Waves

Using a pale blue silk thread, work a row of small back stitches (see page 52) right across the horizon. Ruche a 150mm (6in) length of tubular ribbon on a 100mm (4in) length of double knitting wool, then pin each end of the ribbon just above the right-hand side of the back-stitched horizon.

Starting at the left-hand side, work a row of single Brussels stitch into the back stitches. When you reach the ruched ribbon, enclose the end of the wool, then work spaced stitches over the length of the ribbon, attaching it to the back stitches.

Ruche a 175mm (7in) length of ribbon on a 125mm (5in) length of wool, then pin this at the right-hand side, just under the last row of stitches. Ruche a 125mm (5in) length of ribbon on a 75mm (3in) length of wool, then pin this at the left-hand side. Work a row of single Brussels stitch, from right to left, enclosing the ends of the wool and attaching the lengths of ribbon to the previous row of stitches.

Work another full row of single Brussels stitch, from left to right. Ruche a 150mm (6in) length of tubular ribbon on a 100mm (4in) length of double knitting wool, then pin over the right-hand side of the last row of needlelace. Work another row of single Brussels stitch, from right to left, enclosing the ends of the wool and attaching the lengths of ribbon to the previous row of stitches. Complete the sea by working a few short rows of single Brussels stitch.

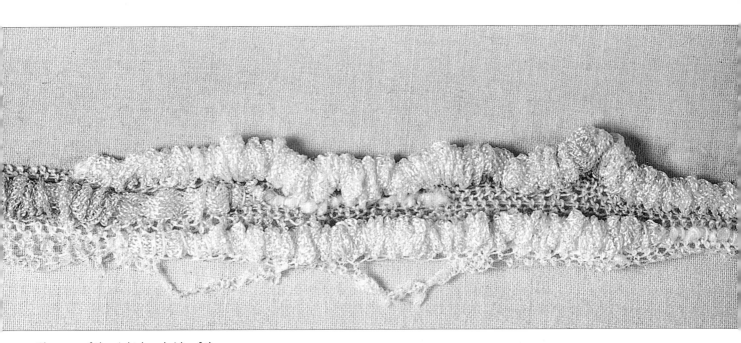

Close-up of the right-hand side of the waves.

Posts

Paint the rough side of a 200mm (8in) square of iron-on interfacing brown, then leave this to dry overnight. Turn the painted surface face down on a piece of lightweight calico, bond the two together with an iron, remove the backing paper, then leave the calico to dry. Cut and fold pieces of card to create two boxes, each 50 x 20 x 6mm (2 x ¾ x ¼in). Use a craft knife to shape the ends of each box. Cut a 6 x 150mm (¼ x 6in) strip of copper sheet, rub shoe polish on the surface to create the appearance of 'rusty metal', then cut it into three 50mm (2in) strips.

Cut two 65 x 50mm (2½ x 2in) pieces of the painted interfaced calico, then glue one piece on each box, tucking the excess into the top end. Glue and wrap one copper strip round one post and two round the other. Working carefully, sew the rear post in position (the front one is attached later).

Rocks

Use the exploded diagram to make pieces of needlelace for rock shapes 3, 5 and 7.

Use fabric paint to colour a 125mm (5in) square piece of interfacing then, when the paint is dry, cut out full-size shapes for rocks 1, 2, 4, 6 and 8–12. Use gold fabric paint or gel pen to draw the shapes of these same rocks on a piece of lightweight calico, allowing 20mm (¾in) round each shape for cutting out. Use a variety of threads to cover each shape with satin stitch (see page 21), then cut them out allowing for turnovers. Stretch each piece of calico over its corresponding piece of interfacing, then lightly glue the turned-over edges to the back of the interfacing.

Stab stitch the bottom edges of rock shape slips 1, 2 and 6 to the background fabric. Referring to page 28, cut three layers of felt for rocks 3, 5 and 7. Apply felt for rock 3 so that it slightly overlaps rock slip 2, then cover it with the corresponding needlelace shape. Stab stitch rock slip 4 to the background fabric, then apply the felt layers and needlelace shapes for rocks 5 and 7. Stab stitch the slips for the remaining rocks.

Carefully sew the front post to the background fabric and rock 4. Cut small pebble shapes from the remains of the painted interfacing, then stab stitch these along the bottom edge of the rocks and around the base of the posts. Sew small beads between these pebbles.

Close-up of bird B5, standing on the needlelace rock.

Birds

Use the exploded diagram to make needlelace pieces (corded single Brussels stitch) for the wing and body shapes for the birds. Bird B5 is double-sided and has two wings, so make extra pieces for this bird.

Cut slightly undersize pieces of felt for birds B1–B4, sew these in position on the background fabric, then fill them with toy stuffing. Sew the needlelace body shapes over the corresponding felt pads, then apply the wings. Use satin stitch to define the legs, feet and beaks, and a small French knot for each eye.

Sew the two body shapes for bird B5 together with small stab stitches, then use the cocktail stick to fill it with toy stuffing. Wrap two very short lengths of wire for the legs and two more for the beak. Apply a dab of PVA to the ends of the legs, then push one end into the padded body and the other into the padded rock. Glue the end of the beak wires then push these, slightly apart, into the head.

Finally, work a few horizontal satin stitches across the beach, around each bird and in front of the rocks to denote rivulets of water.

The finished embroidery.

Figures

In this section, you will learn how to make twenty-first century stumpwork figures, and how to incorporate them into an embroidery. We explain in detail how to make the various components of a figure – limbs, head, face, hair, body shape, clothes and so on – and include detailed, step-by-step instructions for all of the needlelace and embroidery techniques you will need to make clothing and to add details and embellishments to your designs. Four projects are included, each of which shows how to make a different stumpwork figure. Full-size patterns for each of these, as well as the other designs included in this section, are provided at the back of the book.

The templates for these two elegant women can be found on page 167.

Densely worked French knots were used to create the sheep's fleece in this embroidery of a shepherd.

Making arms and legs

Arms and legs are usually made of thin card covered in fine calico (tissue-box card is ideal). Once the shape is made it can be painted with a fabric paint to obtain any skin tone you want. Shown below is the method for making an arm. The same technique is used to make a leg; it is only the shape that differs. If both arms or both legs are visible in your design, you would normally sew one to the background fabric and the other in front of it, freestanding, for a three-dimensional effect.

The footballer's legs were made using the technique shown below. His hands were made using the method described on pages 74–75. The wires were extended to make the arms and wrapped in masking tape for a three-dimensional effect.

1 Cut a piece of thin card from a traced pattern. Use this as the template.

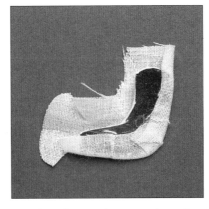

2 Place the template on a piece of fine calico, and cut round it. Make the shape at least 6mm (¼in) wider all round than the card template. Snip around the outside of the calico, from the edge of the calico inwards to the edge of the card.

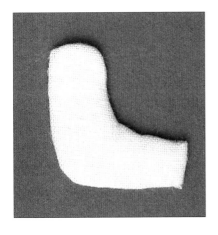

3 Glue the calico to the back of the arm with PVA glue. The arm is now complete and ready for painting or for sewing to the background fabric.

TIP

Make sure the calico is glued to the back of the card only, and not to the front.

Making heads and faces

Heads and faces are fascinating subjects in their own right. In the early days of stumpwork they were made of wood, usually boxwood, and were carved by a carver and supplied to the embroiderer as part of a kit to complete the project.

Today heads are usually made separately from a piece of stuffed calico (a 'slip'), applied to another piece of calico mounted in a ring and then decorated. The following sequence of pictures show how to make faces that are facing forwards. Side-facing ones are treated differently (see page 72). For clarity a blue thread has been used, but normally you would use a colour that matches the fabric.

1 Trace the face outline shape, on the cross of the fabric, on to a piece of fine calico. Make the outline 6mm (¼in) larger than the finished face size you want.

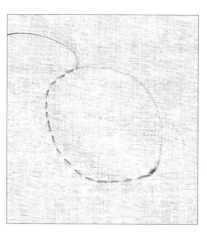

2 Tie a strong knot in the end of a length of sewing thread and make a running stitch around the shape. Leave the end of the thread loose.

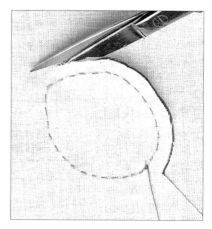

3 Cut around the edge of the shape using a small pair of sharp scissors, approximately 6mm (¼in) outside the gold outline.

4 Start to pull the loose end of the running stitch to create a pouch the size of the face you want.

5 Fill the pouch with toy stuffing. Use a cocktail stick to help push the stuffing in. Pull the pouch tight to the size you want, making sure you keep a pleasing shape to the head, and secure the ends of the running stitch at the back.

These drawings show just some of the facial expressions that can be achieved on stumpwork figures.

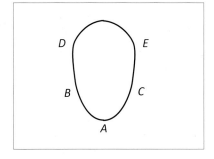

6 Turn the pouch over and position it on another piece of fine calico in an embroidery ring. Starting at A, attach the head shape to the fabric using small, neat, closely worked stab stitches. When you reach point B, go back to A and repeat to C. Return to point B and stitch to D, then go back to C and stitch to E. This pattern of working will help ensure your head remains symmetrical.

7 Push more toy stuffing through the opening at the top until the head is nice and firm. Complete the stitching around the top of the head.

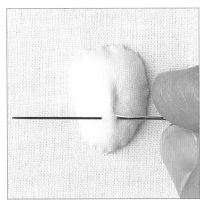

8 To make the nose, thread a needle with sewing thread and put a knot in the end. Pinch the fabric where the nose is to be and pass the needle and thread through the head three or four times. The amount you pull the thread will determine the nose shape.

9 The eyes are made by sewing a detached chain stitch with one strand of cotton in a colour of your choice. Single French knots are used for the coloured parts of the eye. Position the French knots carefully as they help define the expression on the face.

10 The eyebrows and the nostrils are painted on using fabric paint. The mouth is a detached chain stitch using one strand of six-stranded cotton. Shape the mouth according to the expression you want on the face.

Once the felt padding for the hair has been sewn in position (see the next page), the face can be cut out and applied to the background fabric.

TIP

The head is usually the last element to be sewn in place, and once attached it is very difficult to remove. Therefore, it's best to make complete heads as slips, and attach them to the embroidery only when you are totally satisfied with the end result.

Hair styles

Hair styling is a matter of personal choice and ought to be appropriate to the character you are creating. Shown below are just four different methods of hair styling, but they can all be adapted to make the style you choose for your figure. Most styles require you to apply some padding under the stitches to raise the hair away from the face: use a single layer of felt, in a colour that matches the hair colour, sewn in place using stab stitch. Each style is shown half completed, so that you can see the felt padding, and completed to show the final result.

Curly hair is easy to do. Just keep on adding French knots until the felt padding is completely covered.

> **TIP**
> For a forward-facing head, it is often easier to apply the padding before attaching the head to the background. For a side-facing head, the felt padding is applied after the head has been attached to the background fabric.

A balding man is probably the most fiddly to do as the amount of hair is very small. Use white felt and satin stitch over the top.

70

This woman's straight hair was created by placing straight stitches randomly over the felt padding. It is important to get the direction of the stitches right to give the correct look.

TIP

If your figure has long hair, it may need to be sewn on to the background fabric first so that it hangs down behind the figure's clothes.

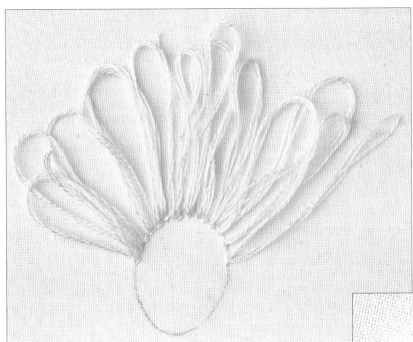

This girl does not need felt padding as there are a lot of stitches to pad the hair out. Use three strands of thread and work a row of long turkey knot stitches around the top of the scalp. Cut the ends of the loops and arrange the hair in whatever style you choose. Trim off any excess hair, and sew on some satin stitches for the fringe.

Side-facing heads

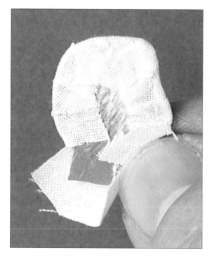

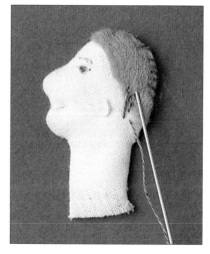

1 Trace the pattern for the head on to a piece of tracing paper. Make sure the neck is long enough to sit behind the body. Cut around the outline of the pattern. Use this as a template to cut out a piece of thin card.

2 Use the card template to cut a piece of fine calico, 6mm (¼in) larger all round than the card shape. Place the card shape in the middle of the calico and snip the calico from its edge to the card all round the head. Apply PVA glue to the back of the card and fold over the edges of the calico carefully to maintain the shape of the head. Do not glue the base of the neck.

3 When the glue has dried push some toy stuffing between the card and the calico via the base of the neck to give the head a rounded appearance. The eye and mouth are made the same way as on the forward-facing head. Apply a piece of felt for the hair padding using stab stitch, and stitch on the hair design (see pages 70–71).

(see pages 70–71).

TIP

The ear is a bullion knot but made slightly differently from a normal bullion knot. Make the windings longer than usual so that they curl round when the needle is withdrawn.

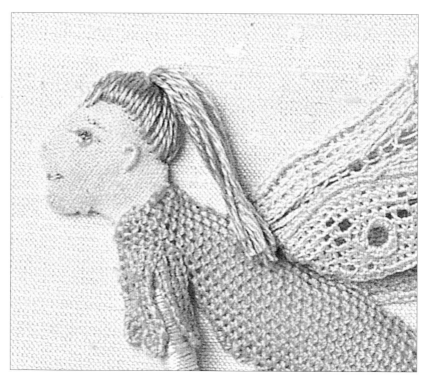

Detail from an embroidery of a fairy kneeling on a toadstool. Notice how her features have been shaped to give her an elfin appearance.

Making different body shapes

To give your stumpwork figures a three-dimensional appearance, add various layers of felt padding underneath their clothes. By varying the size, shape and number of layers, different body shapes can be achieved. Most figures need a single layer of padding sewn over their whole body, with one or two extra layers sewn underneath where required. For example, a woman may need an additional layer of padding around her bust. The toddler in the 'Child Paddling' project on page 76 was given an extra layer of padding around his bottom for extra chubbiness, whereas Uncle Joe, shown here, was made plumper by adding two extra layers of felt padding around his middle (see the pictures below). Alternatively, a little toy stuffing can be used for additional padding.

When building up layers of padding, remember that the top layers need to completely cover the bottom layers, so you will need to make them progressively larger (by approximately 2mm, or $\frac{1}{16}$in, all round). The first layer needs only a few stab stitches to hold it in place. Subsequent layers require more stitches, with the final layer being secured with small, neat, closely worked stitches to create a smooth edge. For each layer, always apply four securing stitches first to hold the shape in place – one at the top, one at the bottom and one at each side – before filling in with the rest of the stitches. To join two pieces of felt padding together, use herringbone cross stitches. This is shown in step 3 below.

Uncle Joe.

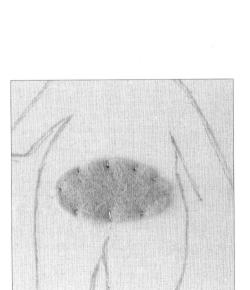

1 Attach the first layer of felt padding around the middle part of the figure. Secure the pad first with four stab stitches then add another four stitches placed between the first ones. This first felt layer should lie well within the gold outline.

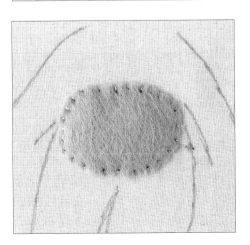

2 Position the second layer of felt over the first one, and secure it with more stab stitches than the first layer.

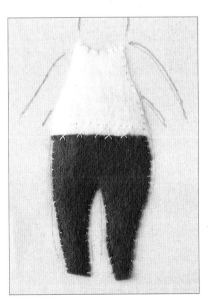

3 Sew on the rest of the padding, covering the upper part of Uncle Joe's body and his legs.

Making hands

We like to make hands that look as realistic as possible. Individual fingers and thumbs are made by wrapping short lengths of paper-covered wire, then these are wrapped together to form palms and wrists. The fingers on the finished hand can then be bent into realistic shapes.

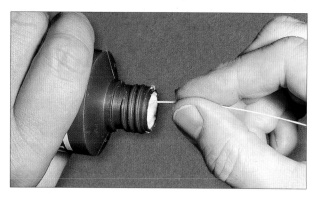

1 Cut the paper-covered wire into five 50mm (2in) lengths (one length for each finger), then dip the end of one finger in PVA glue.

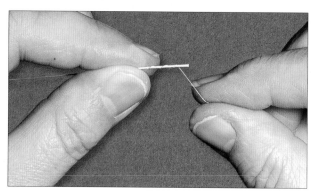

2 Starting approximately 20mm (¾in) from the end, loosely wrap a white thread down to the end of the wire.

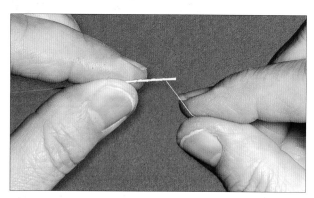

3 Now work back along the wire, closely wrapping the thread for approximately 12mm (½in). Add a little more PVA glue if necessary to secure the thread to the wire. Leave a longish tail of thread on each finger.

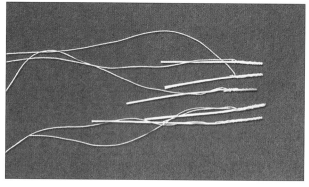

4 Repeat steps 1–3 for each finger and thumb.

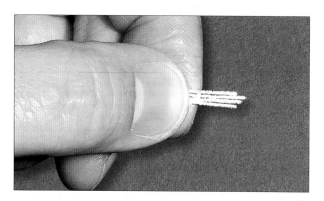

5 Take four fingers, and space them to mimic the length of those on a real hand.

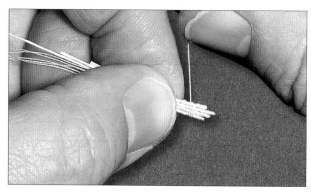

6 Using one of the tails of thread, wrap the four fingers together for three or four turns to start to form the palm.

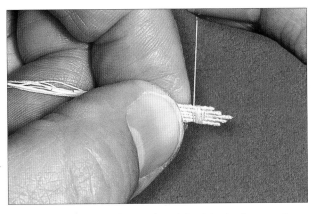

7 Place the wrapped-wire thumb beside the fingers, then continue wrapping thread down the palm.

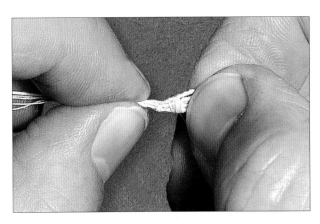

8 When the palm is complete, hold the fingers and thumb flat between two of your fingers, then squeeze the unwrapped wires together to form a wrist.

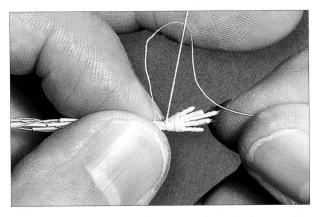

9 Now wrap the wrist and continue along the forearm for approximately 6mm (¼in). Fasten off the wrapping with one or two half-hitch knots, leaving a length of thread.

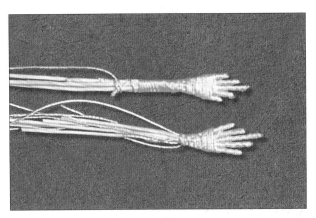

A pair of hands ready to incorporate into an embroidery.

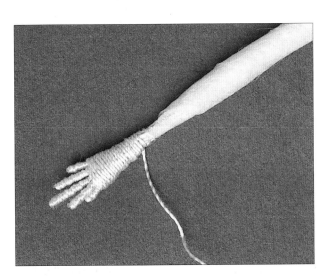

If you have to make a three-dimensional arm, make the wires longer and follow the technique above. Once you have a finished hand, wrap strips of non-woven surgical tape or masking tape around the wires above the wrist. Make the arm more bulky at the top than at the bottom, and make a man's arm thicker than a woman's.

A woman's or child's hand and finger. These were made using a single strand of wire.

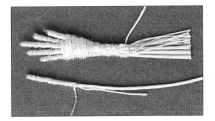

A man's hand and finger. To make a man's finger, start wrapping the wire in the normal way, finishing approximately 6mm (¼in) from the end. Bend the end of the wire back on itself and continue wrapping over both wires. Make up the hand in the normal way.

Child Paddling

The appeal of this little boy paddling could not be ignored, and we just had to reproduce him in stumpwork.

This is a simple project, ideal for those new to creating figures in stumpwork, as there are no hands or face to construct. The feet are hidden by the foaming water. The clothes are all made in needlelace and the foaming water is created using machine embroidery, although it can also be made using French knots (see page 30).

Full-size patterns for the card body parts.

Full-size pattern for the gold outline.

Hair

Back

Bottom second layer

Bottom first layer

Full-size patterns for the felt padding.

1 Attach the silk organza to the silk frame. Make sure it is taut. Paint on an area of blue using fabric paint and a large paintbrush. Allow the paint to dry, then remove the fabric from the frame.

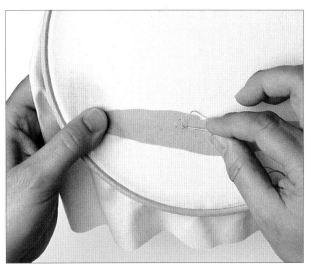

2 Cut out a piece of the blue-painted organza to make the water. Secure the lightweight calico in the embroidery hoop. Choose a suitable position for the water, and attach the organza to the calico using stab stitch in a matching coloured thread.

3 Create the effect of foaming water by machine-stitching with a white thread on to watersoluble fabric. Trace the outline of the foam from the pattern on page 76, leaving two spaces where the boy's legs will be, on to the watersoluble fabric. When you have filled the shape with machine stitching, dissolve the fabric by rinsing it under cold running water, and attach the machine-stitched slip to the central area of the blue-painted organza using stab stitching.

TIP

If you do not have a sewing machine, you can make the white foam using French knots (see page 30) embroidered straight on to the organza.

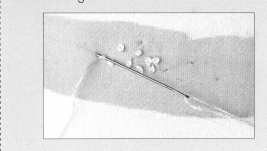

4 Remove the calico from the hoop and trace on the pattern using gold gel pen. Replace the calico in the hoop, this time with a backing of medium-weight calico. Make sure the fabric is taut, and that the picture is positioned centrally in the ring.

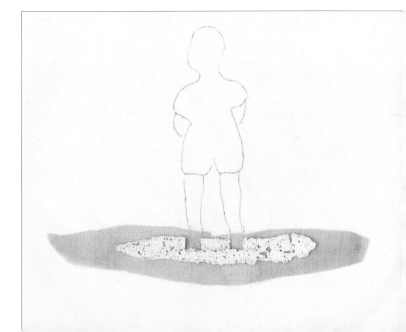

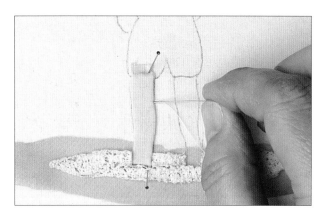

5 Make the limbs and neck using the patterns on page 76. Follow the technique described on page 67. Taking each part in turn, first pin it to the background fabric then sew it in place using stab stitches.

TIP

Always make sure the legs are sufficiently long for the tops of them to be hidden under the figure's skirt or shorts.

The figure, with all the body pieces (apart from the head) in place.

6 Using the templates on page 76, cut out the shapes for the felt padding. To give the bottom a more rounded appearance, two layers of felt are used. Attach the first layer of padding to the boy's bottom using stab stitch.

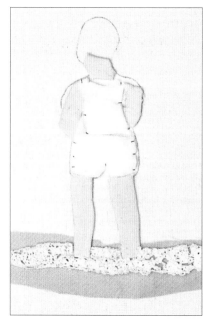

7 Attach the second layer of felt to the boy's bottom, and the single layer to his back. Use stab stitch, as before.

Needlelace

Make sure the patterns fit the child in your embroidery before making the needlelace, and adapt them if necessary.

Make all the needlelace using corded single Brussels stitch in colours of your choice using the patterns shown opposite. Take note of the direction of working.

Use top stitching along the bottom of the sleeves, the neckline of the boy's top, and the neckline and bottom of his dungarees.

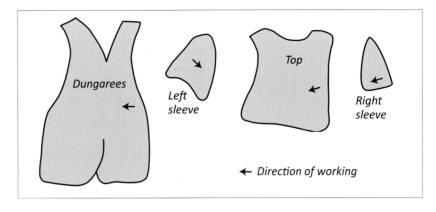

Dungarees

Left sleeve

Top

Right sleeve

← *Direction of working*

8 Sew the sleeves over the calico-covered card arms first, followed by the back of the boy's top. Use the same thread as you used to make the needlelace.

TIP

When you are making a piece of needlelace, leave long threads and use these to sew the lace to your embroidery.

9 Attach the dungarees to the figure.

10 Make the head, using the template on page 76 and following the method shown on pages 68–69, and attach it to your embroidery, Finally, add short blond hair using long satin stitches (see page 21). Use a modified bullion knot to make the ear – see the fairy on page 72.

The completed project.

To complement the little boy, we have used the same techniques to make a little girl paddling. Notice how the slightly chubbier legs make her look younger. The foaming water in this picture was made using French knots, and the girl's hair was made using long turkey knot stitches (see page 22). The skirt was made slightly fuller than the pattern so that it lay in natural folds when it was sewn to the background fabric. To add a petticoat, attach some lace to a separate piece of cloth and sew it on to your embroidery before attaching the skirt.

The Fairy

This enchanting figure is challenging but not impossible, even for a beginner. The same rules for making needlelace apply to the shapes in this project as they do to any other. They do, however, need a little more patience and concentration. To help, an enlarged cordonnet outline for the right wing and detailed instructions on how to make it are provided on page 84; the left wing is simply a mirror image of the right wing. The cordonnets for the skirt and bodice are straightforward. For the body parts, follow the same methods as outlined earlier – the only difficult part is connecting the hands to the ends of the arms. If you can work through these difficult parts the rest is fairly straightforward and the end result is extremely satisfying.

as provided on page 84

Materials

- Embroidery hoop, 250mm (10in)
- Needlelace pad(s) (see page 38)
- Dupion silk, 350mm (14in) square
- Lightweight calico, 350mm (14in) square
- Medium-weight calico, 350mm (14in) square
- 100/3 embroidery silk
- Sewing thread
- No. 9 embroidery needle
- No. 9 sharps needle
- Dressmakers' pins
- Scissors
- Fabric paint and small paintbrush
- Tracing paper
- Pencil
- Gold gel pen
- PVA glue
- Thin card
- Felt for padding
- Toy stuffing
- Cocktail stick
- Tweezers
- Paper-covered wire
- Fine copper wire
- Gold-coloured metallic thread
- Gold stars

Full-size pattern for the gold outline.

Needlelace

Wings

The wings are the first element to be attached to the figure, so you should begin by making these. The instructions for making the cordonnet for the fairy's wings are given on page 84. To start the needlelace, begin with a row of buttonhole stitches across the top of the shape and work a couple of rows. When you get to the hole at the top of the wing, work down the wing on the left-hand side until you reach the bottom edge of the hole. Work a straight line across to the right-hand side of the wing, and then go back up on the right-hand side until you are level with the top of the hole. You can then continue working down the shape in the normal way. Once the needlelace is complete, finish with top stitching around the outside of the wing, the purple area inside the wing and the hole.

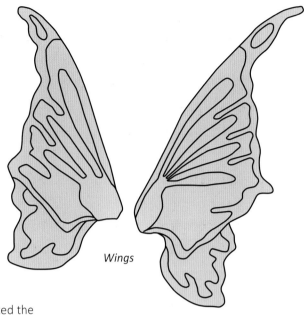

Wings

Clothes

It is better to make the fairy's clothes after you have completed the padding on her body (step 11 in the project). You can then make sure the patterns provided are the right size for your embroidery and adapt them if necessary.

Make the bodice and skirt using corded single Brussels stitch in colours of your choice. Take note of the direction of working. Use top stitching around the neckline and the hem of the skirt. Incorporate a length of fine copper wire into the hem of the skirt so that it can be bent into shape.

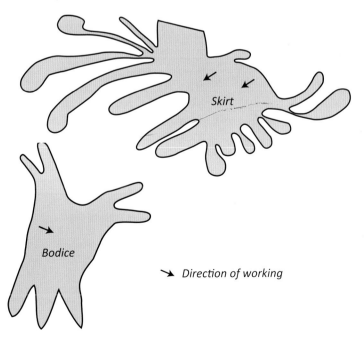

Skirt

Bodice

➤ *Direction of working*

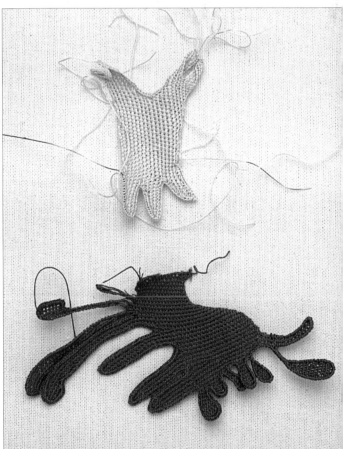

Making the cordonnet for the fairy's wing

> ⟩ *Direction of couching with two threads*
> ⟨⟩ *Single thread one way, two threads on the way back*
> ↘ *Direction of working*

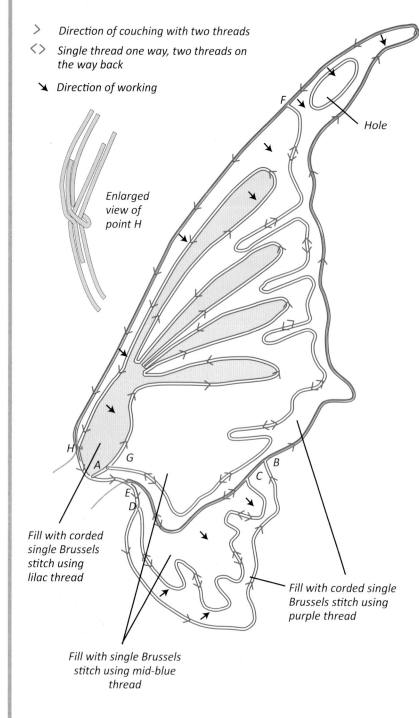

Enlarged view of point H

Hole

Fill with corded single Brussels stitch using lilac thread

Fill with corded single Brussels stitch using purple thread

Fill with single Brussels stitch using mid-blue thread

The cordonnet for the fairy's wing may seem complicated, but the basic rules apply. Two unbroken threads are couched down round the design to support the filling stitches. A fine copper wire is added to the outside edge to enable the top of the wing to be bent away from the background fabric.

Start with a loop at A. One side of the loop will need to be twice as long as the other. Couch down in the direction of the arrows around the lilac-coloured central pattern back to A. When you get to A, using a small crochet hook or a large-eyed needle, take one thread through the loop you started with. Continue round the bottom of the wing, following the arrows to B. At B take one thread to C. At C take the single thread round clockwise to D, then back again to C. Remember to couch down the single thread with a few stitches to hold it in place, and to couch down normally on the way back over both threads.

When you get back to C take your single thread round to E. At E add a fine copper wire (leave a tail of 50mm, or 2in) as you couch both threads back to B. At B pick up the other thread you left behind and couch both threads and the wire round to F. At F take one of the threads round to G, couching down in a number of places to hold it in position. At G return to F, couching down both threads. When you get back to F pick up the thread and the wire and couch down to H. At H follow the enlarged diagram to finish the cordonnet. Leave 20mm (¾in) of the wire as a tail to be sewn down later. The hole at the top is a normal cordonnet.

Patterns for card body parts

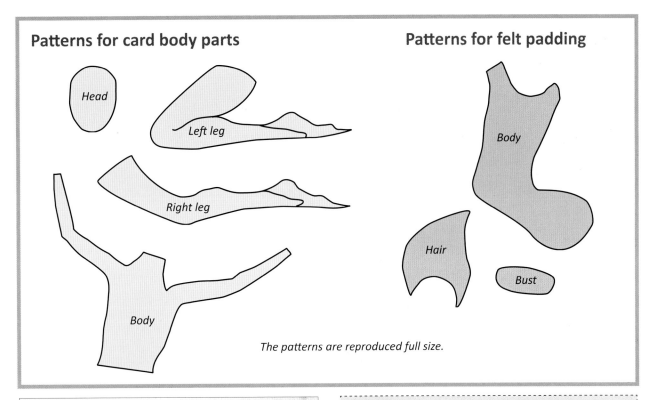

Head

Left leg

Right leg

Body

Patterns for felt padding

Body

Hair

Bust

The patterns are reproduced full size.

TIP

When you are tracing the pattern, make sure you transfer the outline only — not the details.

1 Begin by tracing the pattern for the fairy on to the dupion using gold gel pen. Place the fabric in the hoop with a backing of medium-weight calico and tighten the hoop so that the fabric is taut. Make sure the pattern is positioned centrally in the hoop.

2 Attach the wings to the background fabric using stab stitch. Attach only the inner part of the wing; raise the outer parts so that they stand away from the background, giving a three-dimensional feel to the image.

85

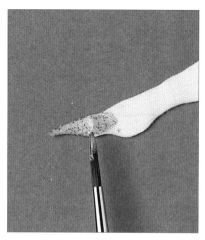

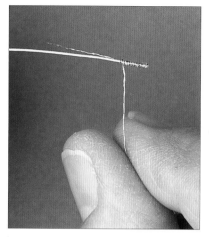

3 Make the two legs using the patterns on page 85. Follow the instructions provided on page 67. On each leg, draw on the outline of the shoe lightly in pencil, and then paint the shoe on using fabric paint and a small paintbrush.

4 For each shoe decoration, dip the end of a length of fine paper-covered wire into PVA glue. Before the glue has time to dry, take a length of gold-coloured metallic thread and wind it tightly round the end of the wire. Secure the thread, leaving a long end with which to attach the decoration to the shoe.

5 Coil the end of each decoration by holding it firmly in a pair of tweezers and forming it into the correct shape.

6 Attach a decoration to the back of each shoe, sewing it in place using the long end of the gold thread.

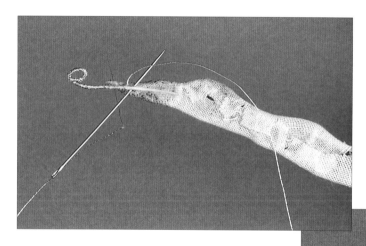

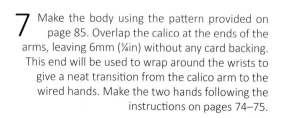

7 Make the body using the pattern provided on page 85. Overlap the calico at the ends of the arms, leaving 6mm (¼in) without any card backing. This end will be used to wrap around the wrists to give a neat transition from the calico arm to the wired hands. Make the two hands following the instructions on pages 74–75.

8 Attach the two legs to the picture using stab stitch.

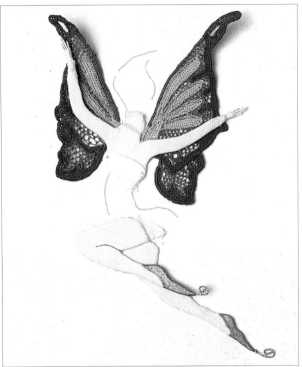

9 Attach the arms and body to the picture using stab stitch. Cut out a piece of felt padding for the fairy's bust using the pattern on page 85, and sew it in place.

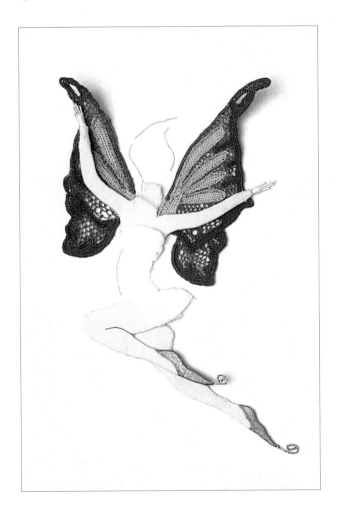

10 Cut out the felt padding for the fairy's body and attach it to the background fabric. Use stab stitch.

11 Attach the fairy's skirt and bodice using the long threads left on the needlelace.

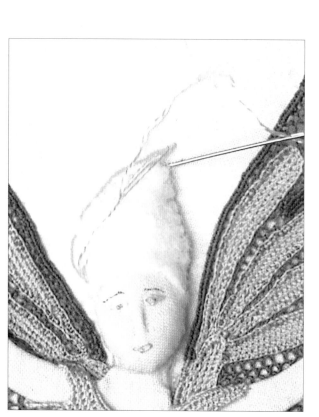

12 Make the fairy's face following the techniques described on pages 68–69 and attach it to the picture. Cut out and attach the felt padding for the hair.

13 Using a single strand of cotton and an embroidery needle, construct the hair using long satin stitch.

The completed project. The gold stars add a touch of magic to the finished piece!

Gone Fishing

This delightful picture was inspired by Kay's dad who, during his lifetime, loved fishing. To make the picture more appealing we have made the figure into a young boy.

The foreground leaves of the bulrushes and all of the boy's clothing are made of needlelace, except for the boy's shoes which are made of leather. The filling stitch used in the needlelace is corded single Brussels stitch. Satin stitch is used for the boy's hair and over interfacing for the background leaves of the bulrushes. The bulrush heads are made using turkey knot stitch and the stems are worked in raised stem band stitch. The worm escaping from the tin can is a single drizzle stitch, and the water is a piece of fine silk chiffon painted the same colour as the background fabric.

Full-size pattern for the gold outline.

Materials

- Embroidery hoop, 250mm (10in)
- Two silk frames
- Needlelace pad(s) (see page 38)
- Lightweight calico, 300mm (12in) square
- Medium-weight calico, 300mm (12in) square
- Silk chiffon, 100 x 200mm (4 x 8in)
- Stranded cotton or 100/3 embroidery silk
- Sewing thread
- No. 9 embroidery needle
- No. 9 sharps needle
- No. 10 ballpoint needle
- Dressmakers' pins
- Scissors
- Fabric paint and large paintbrush
- Blue acrylic paint
- Tracing paper
- Pencil
- Gold gel pen
- PVA glue
- Superglue
- Thin card
- Felt for padding
- Non-woven surgical tape
- Toy stuffing
- Cocktail stick
- Fine copper wire

For the shoes:
- Gloving leather
- Black cotton thread

For the boat and the float:
- 5mm (¼in) balsa wood
- Wood veneer
- Acrylic paints

For the rod and line:
- Cocktail stick
- 3mm (⅛in) wooden dowel or a button
- Fine fishing line

For the tin can:
- Foil

Making the body parts and padding

Before you begin to construct the fisherman, make all the card body parts and put them to one side ready to incorporate into your picture. Use the templates below to make the head and two legs, and cut two layers of padding for the body, one for the right arm and one for the hair.

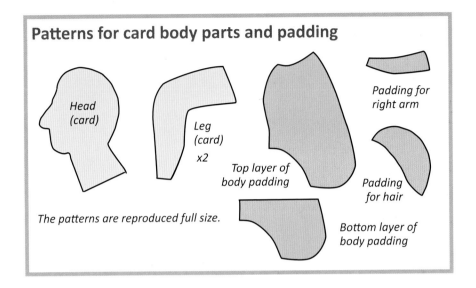

Patterns for card body parts and padding

Head (card)

Leg (card) x2

Top layer of body padding

Padding for right arm

Padding for hair

Bottom layer of body padding

The patterns are reproduced full size.

Making the clothes

It is advisable to wait until step 7 of the project, when all the padding, the right arm and the right leg are in place, before making the clothes. You can then check that the patterns provided are the right size for your fisherman, and adjust them if necessary. You will, however, need to make one of the socks early on and sew it to the right leg before attaching the leg to the background (step 3).

The fisherman's shirt, shorts, cap and socks are made of needlelace, and his shoes are made of leather. Trace the pattern for the shoes on to tracing paper and cut it out. Use this as a template to cut out two shoe shapes and one reversed shoe shape from gloving leather. One of these will be used for the right foot and two for the left foot, one glued on each side, to give it a three-dimensional appearance.

TIP

If you are designing clothes for a stumpwork figure, think about what they would wear in real life and dress your figure the same way.

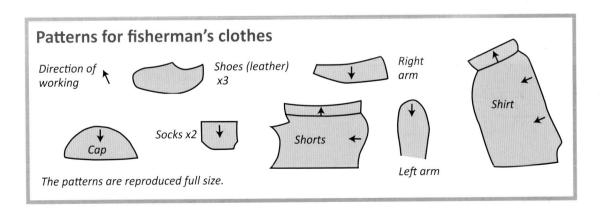

Patterns for fisherman's clothes

Direction of working

Shoes (leather) x3

Right arm

Cap

Socks x2

Shorts

Left arm

Shirt

The patterns are reproduced full size.

Needlelace

Use the patterns on the previous page and follow the notes below to make the cordonnets and the needlelace parts using corded single Brussels stitch. In general, when applying needlelace to a stumpwork design, no top stitching is required prior to releasing the lace from the pad, except where the edges show – in this case the cap edge, the edge of the collar and the waistband and edges of the shorts.

The left arm is freestanding and only the top of the arm is attached to the background. The left sleeve is therefore constructed around the arm before it is attached to the picture, and the instructions for this are given on pages 96–97.

Remember to check the sizes of the patterns before you start working. The patterns provided here are for the parts we made and yours may be different in size or tension. The needlelace parts were all made on a single needlelace pad, though you can make a separate pad for each one. The letters refer to the notes below.

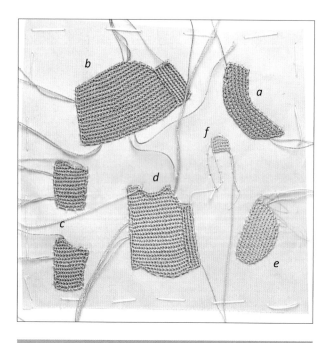

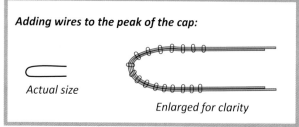

Adding wires to the peak of the cap:

Actual size

Enlarged for clarity

a. Right sleeve

The right sleeve is worked in corded single Brussels stitch.

b. Shirt

The shirt is worked in corded single Brussels stitch. Note the directions of working for the collar and body section. The collar is top stitched on the front edge and bottom only. Turn the collar over before applying it to the background fabric. The shirt is longer than it needs to be so that it can be 'tucked into' the shorts that are then fitted over the top of it.

c. Socks

The socks are made using corded single Brussels stitch with no top stitching.

d. Shorts

The shorts are worked in corded single Brussels stitch. Work the bottom part first starting at the back and working down to the leg. Turn the lace round and work the waistband from the bottom to the top. Working this way will give a neat edge to the bottom of the waistband.

Apply top stitching across the top of the waistband and around the leg. Do not stitch the shorts into position until you have completed both legs.

e. Cap

The main part of the cap is worked in straightforward corded single Brussels stitch and then top stitched along the bottom.

f. Peak of cap

The peak of the cap is a little complicated. On your needlelace pad lay a fine wire in a U shape and couch it down.

Starting at the tip of the peak, work corded single Brussels stitch across the U shape. Continue for the length you want the peak. The one shown has eight rows. Release the lace from the pad, feed the back wire into the front of the cap and sew off. The other wire will eed into the head at the base of the cap approximately 6mm (¼in) from the front.

TIP

When positioning the gold outline on the background fabric, leave enough room to the left of the fisherman for his rod and float.

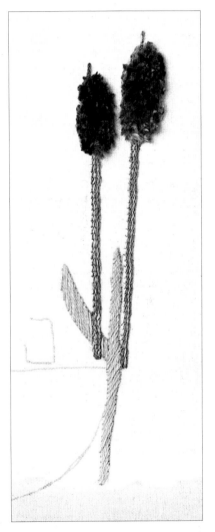

1 Stretch a 300mm (12in) square of lightweight calico in a silk frame. Dampen the lower part of the calico with clean water, then lay a wash of pale blue and allow it to dry. When laying the wash, allow enough room on the left-hand side for the fisherman's rod. Stretch the piece of silk chiffon in another frame and paint it with the same colour blue. This will be the last element you add to your picture.

When the paint is dry, remove the calico from the frame and trace the pattern using the gold gel pen. Place the fabric in the embroidery hoop with a backing of medium-weight calico, and tighten the hoop so that the fabric is taut.

2 Work the bulrushes using raised stem stitch band for the stems and turkey knot stitch for the heads. Use two short straight stitches for the top of the bulrush heads. The background leaves are satin stitch over interfacing, which is ideal for recreating the crisp edges of the leaves and helps give the satin stitch a neater appearance. Paint the interfacing to match the thread colour to minimise the white show-through.

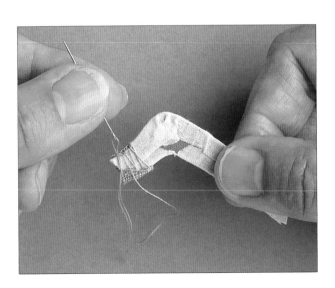

3 Wrap one of the socks around the bottom of the right leg, and lace the two edges together on the back. Attach the other sock to the left leg and put it to one side.

4 Sew the right leg to the picture using stab stitch. Attach the two layers of padding to the fisherman's body.

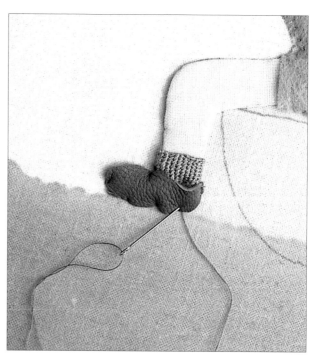

5 Attach the right shoe to the right leg using very small, neat stab stitches. Use a sharp needle to help pierce the leather.

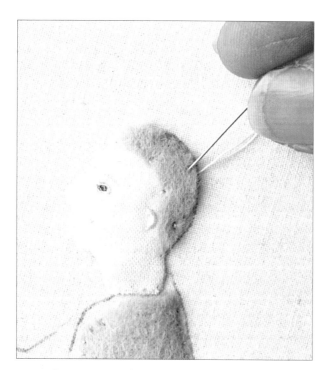

6 Make a head using the pattern on page 91, and sew it to the background fabric (see pages 68–69). Add a layer of padding for the fisherman's hair.

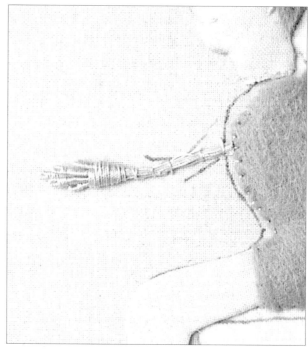

7 Make the right arm and hand following the technique described on pages 74–75. The arm should be as long as the fisherman's shirt sleeve (approximately 20mm, or ¾in, from the wrist to the body). Couch the arm down, as far as the wrist, to the background fabric.

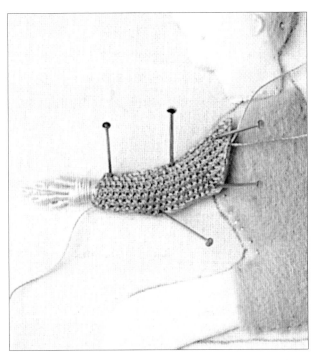

8 Attach a layer of felt padding over the wires and stab stitch it into place, then sew on the fisherman's right sleeve.

9 Sew on the fisherman's shirt.

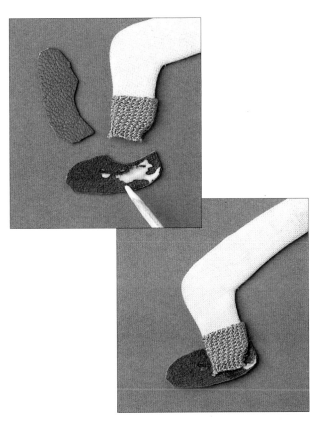

10 Take the left leg and two shoe shapes (one reversed) that you prepared earlier, and glue the reversed shoe shape to the right side of the foot using PVA glue.

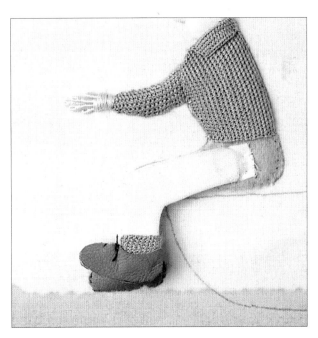

11 Glue the other shoe shape to the left side of the foot to complete the shoe. Thread a short length of black cotton through the top of the shoe and tie it in a knot to make the shoelace. Attach the left leg to the picture using stab stitch. Sew only around the top of the leg, underneath the area covered by the shorts, leaving the rest free to dangle.

12 Now the left leg is in place the shorts can be stitched on over the leg and the bottom of the shirt.

Constructing the left arm

First, make a man's hand following the instructions on pages 74–75, leaving tails of wire about 50mm (2in) long. Cut 80mm (3¼in) strips of non-woven surgical tape and wrap them around the lengths of wire to form the arm, making it slightly fatter at the top than at the wrist. Paint the arm with blue acrylic paint and leave it to dry.

13 Using the pattern on page 91, set up a needlelace pad and couch a 150mm (6in) length of embroidery silk, doubled, on to the pad.

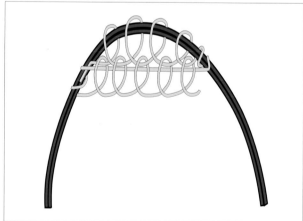

14 Make a foundation row of buttonhole stitches across the top of the cordonnet, and lay the thread back across the row. Make a buttonhole stitch into the first loop of the row above, but *do not pick up the laid thread*. Make the next stitch in the same way, and continue across the row. Repeat for six rows.

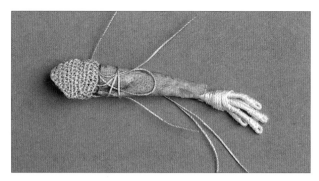

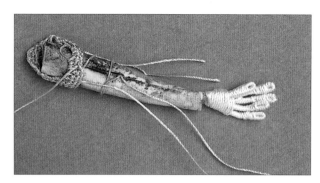

15 Carefully remove the needlelace from the pad and lay it over the arm so that the needlelace covers the top of the wires. Wrap the needle and thread around the arm twice – this will help to hold the needlelace in place.

16 Starting at the front of the arm, work one row of buttonhole stitches into the loops of the row above. Continue around the arm, working buttonhole stitches into the two threads that were wound around the arm. After working two or three rows, make sure the arm fits comfortably on to the body of the fisherman. Continue round the arm, working buttonhole stitches into the loops of the previous row, until the needlelace covers the arm.

17 Attach the left arm by stab stitching around the top part of the arm only. Carefully bend the fingers round as if they were holding the fishing rod.

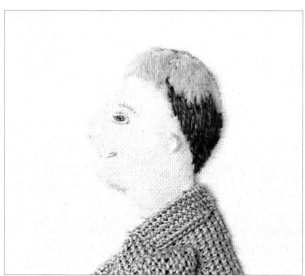

18 Sew on the hair using long satin stitch.

19 Attach the cap then the peak of the cap, as described on page 92.

Making the fishing rod, reel, line, float, tin can and boat

The fishing rod

The fishing rod is made from a cocktail stick with the pointed ends cut off.

The reel

The reel is a 3mm (1/8in) length of 5mm (1/4in) dowel glued with PVA to the cocktail stick. The handle of the reel is a piece of cocktail stick inserted into a hole drilled in the reel.

The line

For the line, a 400mm (16in) length of fine fishing line was tied to the rod in four places. A small amount of superglue was applied to each knot to stop it from coming undone. The line was hung in loops between each knot.

The float

The float was cut from balsa wood and painted using acrylic paints.

The tin can

For the tin can cut a piece of foil 10 x 20mm (1/2 x 3/4in) and bend it to the shape of the can:

Paint the can in a colour of your choice using acrylic paint. When the paint is dry, glue the can in position on the background fabric using PVA glue. The worm is made using drizzle stitch, see page 173. Bend the worm over the top of the can and secure it with a small dab of PVA glue.

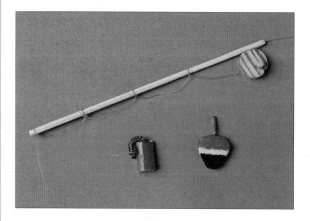

The boat

To make the boat, cut a piece of 5mm (1/4in) balsa wood to the shape of the template below.

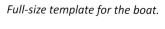

Full-size template for the boat.

Cut a piece of veneer across the grain 5mm (1/4in) wide and 100mm (4in) long. The veneer is cut across the grain to make it easier to go round the curve of the boat. Attach the veneer to the curved edge of the boat using PVA glue and hold it in place with your fingers until the glue goes off, or secure it with elastic bands until the glue has set.

Attaching the veneer to the edge of the boat.

When the glue is dry, trim the top edges flush with the top of the boat. Cut another piece of veneer, this time with the grain, 5mm (1/4in) wide and 60mm (2½in) long, and glue it to the top edge of the boat, overlapping the edge on each side. When the glue is dry, trim it flush to the sides of the boat.

Use the boat as a template to cut the veneer for the front of the boat. It doesn't matter if you cut the veneer oversize as it can be sanded back to the correct size later. Glue the veneer to the front of the boat.

The completed boat.

Needlelace bulrush leaves

Work each leaf in corded single Brussels stitch. Top stitch around the edge of each leaf but not along the bottom. Add a fine copper wire to the cordonnet as it is couched down so that the leaves can be bent away from the background fabric and moulded into interesting shapes. For each leaf, measure off a length of 100/3 embroidery silk and fold it in half. Cut a single length of fine copper wire, enough to go round the leaf plus 50mm (2in). Start to couch just the thread along the bottom of the leaf, then add in the wire, leaving a 25mm (1in) tail of wire, on the corner. Couch the threads and wire round to the other corner, leave the wire and finish couching the threads along the bottom of the leaf.

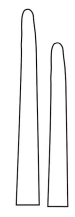

Full-size patterns for the bulrush leaves.

20 Attach the leaves to the background fabric by taking the wires through to the back of your work and sewing them in place. Bend the leaves into interesting shapes. Hold the fishing rod in place with a couple of stitches, then arrange the hands so that they look as if they are holding the rod and winding the reel. Position the float so that it appears half submerged in the water and secure it with a stitch around the top. Attach the end of the line to the background fabric, just behind the float, with a spot of PVA glue. Finally, position the boat and the tin can, securing them both with PVA glue.

TIP

Before completing your picture, you may need to reposition it within the embroidery hoop so that there is enough room to the left of the fisherman for his rod and line.

21 Lay the blue-painted chiffon prepared in step 1 across the bottom of the picture so that it lies over the float and the bottom of the boat but not over the fisherman's shoes. Hold it in place with a few stitches.

The completed project.

The Gardener

This picture of a man working in his garden includes lots of techniques, most of which are covered in the other projects in this book. If you want to make this embroidery, feel free to copy it exactly. Alternatively, you could use it as the basis for a more personal composition, and, say, depict the plants in your own garden. Here, long and short stitch, French knots, satin stitch, raised stem stitch band, bullion knots, back stitch and corded single Brussels stitch are used to complete the embroidery.

Materials

- Needlelace pads (see page 38)
- Crochet thread No. 80
- Sewing thread
- Lightweight calico for the background fabric and slips
- Fabric paints and brushes
- Silk fabric
- Iron-on interfacing
- Salt
- Cotton moulds
- Six-stranded cotton
- 100/3 silk thread
- No. 9 sharps needle
- No.10 ballpoint needle
- No. 24 tapestry needle
- Fine wire
- Paper-covered wire
- Acrylic paint
- Beads: fruit, vegtables and flower centres
- Toy stuffing
- Cocktail stick
- Felt for padding
- Double-knitting wool
- Tubular ribbon
- Organza
- Air-drying clay
- Cocktail stick
- Stiletto
- PVA glue
- Wood glue
- Metallic paint
- Leather
- Watering-can button

Enlarge this diagram to 150% to create a full-size pattern.

101

Painting the background

Paint the background (see page 63). Here a blue wash is used for the sky, a green wash for the grass and a brown wash for the earth. Leave a 'dry line' along the horizon and allow the sky wash to bleed down to this edge. Create the soft edge between the grass and earth by applying the brown wash while the green one is still damp. Leave the fabric to dry, then fix the colours with an iron.

Referring to the full-size pattern, use gold fabric paint or gel pen to outline the shape of the gardener, the snail, the topiary and the tree trunk.

Espalier tree

This tree consists of lengths of paper-covered wire wrapped with silk and decorated with small beads. As you wrap the individual branches with silk, incorporate another type of thread and leave small loops to suggest leaves, and add the bead fruit along the length of the branch. Wrap the bottom ends of the branches together to form the trunk. Try to copy nature and make the finished trunk and the branches somewhat knobbly. Bend the branches to shape, then couch the tree on to the background fabric.

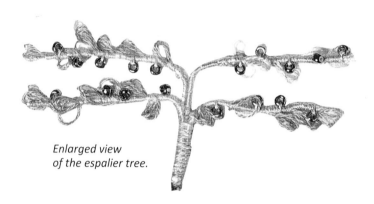

*Enlarged view
of the espalier tree.*

Cauliflowers and cabbage

There are six leaves on each of the two cauliflowers and on the cabbage. Each leaf is made from two layers of painted silk fabric, bonded together with iron-on interfacing, so the piece of silk needs to be large enough to provide thirty-six leaf shapes. Using a suitable shade of green, paint the silk fabric. When it is completely dry, cut it in half, then bond the two pieces together with iron-on interfacing.

Using the diagram right as a guide, back stitch the outlines of each leaf and its veins on the silk. Carefully cut out each leaf, just beyond the stitches then, overlapping them slightly, stitch six leaves together on the background fabric.

Make a slip of French knots (see page 30) for the centre of each cauliflower, then sew these in the middle of the sets of leaves.

Paint a small piece of silk fabric dark green for the heart of the cabbage. While the paint is still wet, lightly sprinkle salt over the silk to create texture. When the silk is completely dry, brush off the salt, select an interesting area, then cut out a 50mm (2in) circle. Gather the fabric round a cotton mould, secure with a few oversewn stitches then trim off the excess fabric. Sew the finished cabbage heart to the circle of leaves.

*Use this full-size
diagram as a guide
to cut the leaves for
the cabbage and
cauliflowers. Vary the
shape slightly for each
leaf, but keep them all
at the same scale.*

*Enlarged views of the cabbage
and one of the cauliflowers.*

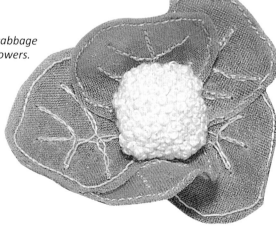

Pear tree

Working in the gold outline on the background fabric, use raised stem stitch band (see page 33) to embroider the tree trunk.

Use the cordonnet diagram to make fourteen needlelace leaves, using your choice of filling stitch. Reinforcing the outline of six leaves with fine wire, top stitch all round each leaf.

Use acrylic paint to colour pear-shaped beads. You could use medium-sized, round beads as apples or oranges.

Sew the nine background leaves to the background fabric. Here, leaves 1, 2 and 8 are not wired and are sewn all round, whereas the other six are wired and are attached at their bases. Arrange the remaining five unwired leaves in a star-shape then secure this in the middle of the tree. Do not worry if these leaves curl up, they look quite natural this way.

Sew on the fruit beads then, finally, shape the freestanding parts of the wired leaves to make them look natural.

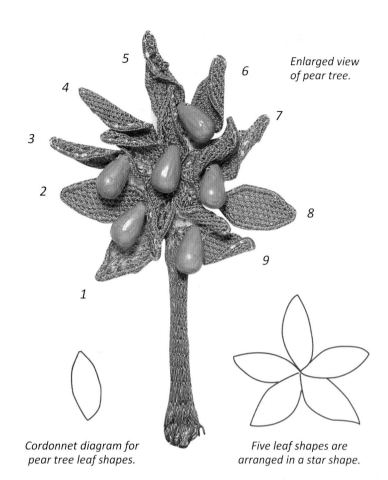

Enlarged view of pear tree.

Cordonnet diagram for pear tree leaf shapes.

Five leaf shapes are arranged in a star shape.

Currants

Use the cordonnet diagram to make four needlelace leaf shapes, filling them with corded single Brussels stitch. Top stitch round the whole of each leaf shape.

The six currants are wrapped pebble beads. Using a long length of silk and a ballpoint needle, take the thread through the hole and round the outside of the bead until it is completely covered. Make joins by leaving all tails at one end of the bead (the base of the currant).

The tuft at the top of each currant is a short length of all strands of six-stranded cotton. Secure it by bringing a silk thread up through the bead, over the six strands and back down again. Trim the tuft to size.

Use one strand of six-stranded cotton to make the stalks. Tie a knot round all threads at the base of the currant, wrap the cotton thread round the other threads for approximately 12mm (½in), then fasten off.

Wrap a 40mm (1½in) length of paper-covered wire to make each stem. Incorporate the currants and leaves as you wrap the wire. Couch the base of the stems to the background fabric.

Full-size cordonnet diagram for currant leaf shapes.

Enlarged view of currants.

103

Onions and carrots

The onions are small wooden beads sewn to the background fabric. Bring a cotton thread up through the fabric and the bead, take it over the bead and back down into the background fabric – repeat four or five times to securely attach the bead.

Cut a 150mm (6in) length of thread, wrap half of it round your finger, slip the loops off the finger and oversew the bottom of the loops twice. Now take the loose end of thread down through the bead and the background fabric, pull it firmly to draw part of the loops into the top of the bead, then fasten off on the back. Cut the loops in half to make the onion leaves.

The carrots are 3mm (1/8in) diameters of padded satin stitch (see page 35) sewn on to the background fabric. Wrap a 100mm (4in) length of cotton thread round your finger, slip the loops off the finger, oversew them on top of the padded satin stitch, then cut the loops to form the leaves.

Enlarged view of onions and carrots.

Marrow

Use the cordonnet diagrams to make the needlelace pieces for the marrow and the leaf.

Work the marrow shape as one piece. Fill the whole shape with a dark green corded single Brussels stitch, looping the stitches round the dividing lines. When the filling is complete, top stitch along the dividing lines with a pale green (do not top stitch round the outside edges). Release the needlelace, then sew the sides of the shape together to form a tube, leaving one end open. Fill the tube with toy stuffing using a cocktail stick, then close the end to complete the marrow.

Work the leaf segments in your choice of stitches, then top stitch round the outer edge. Sew the leaf to the background fabric, then secure one end of the marrow with a few stitches.

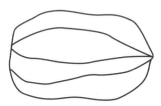

Full-size cordonnet diagram for the marrow. Work the shape as one piece, incorporating the cordonnet threads for the segments into the loops of the filling stitches.

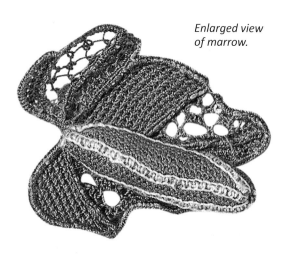

Enlarged view of marrow.

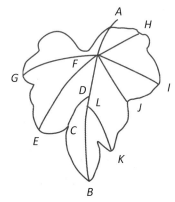

Full-size cordonnet diagram for the marrow leaf. This is rather more complex than many of the other cordonnets used in this book, but it is built up in a similar way to the leaf shape on page 39. Start with the loop in the cordonnet thread at point A, take both threads across to B and round to C. Take one thread up to D and back again, then take both threads round to E. Take one thread up to F and back again, then take both threads round to G. Continue working round the shape, using the double thread round the outer edge and taking one thread into the centre and back again for the side veins. At point K, take one thread down to B and back again, then take both threads to point L to finish the cordonnet.

104

Strawberries

Four of the five strawberries are worked over stuffed felt, and consist of a decorated layer of needlelace. The freestanding strawberry comprises two decorated layers of needlelace, sewn together, then padded with toy stuffing.

Cut lengths of a pale gold thread, arrange them on the background fabric to represent straw, then couch them down with one or two stitches.

Referring to the pattern and the cordonnet diagram for the strawberry, cut four slightly undersized pieces of felt. Secure these to the background fabric, then pad them out with toy stuffing. Use the cordonnet diagram to make six pieces of needlelace for the strawberries, filling each one with corded single Brussels stitch (see page 40). Before releasing these from the backing material, work a decorative layer of detached chain stitch into the needlelace. Then, using gold thread, make a small stitch over the securing stitch of the chain for the pips. Do not top stitch these pieces of needlelace. Sew four of the shapes over the padded felt. Sew the other two pieces together to make the freestanding strawberry, then pad this berry with toy stuffing.

Use the cordonnet diagram for the calyx to make six pieces of needlelace, filling each shape with corded single Brussels stitch. Top stitch round each shape, then remove it from the backing material. Secure the top edge of one shape to each of the padded-felt strawberries and two shapes to the freestanding berry.

Wrap two lengths of paper-covered wire for the stalks. Secure one length to the freestanding strawberry, then take the other end of this through the background fabric and fasten off. Couch the other stalk across the top of the padded strawberries.

Use gold fabric paint or gel pen to draw three leaf shapes on a piece of lightweight calico, spacing them slightly apart. Couch a length of fine wire round each leaf shape and down the centre vein, leaving a short tail at the base of each leaf. Fill in the shape with long and short stitch (see page 24). Buttonhole round the outside of each leaf and along the central veins. Define the side veins with straight stitches. Cut out each leaf, gather the wire tails together, then wrap them securely. Use a stiletto to make a hole in the background fabric, take the tail through and fasten it on the back.

Full-size cordonnet diagrams for the strawberry and the calyx.

Full-size diagram for the leaf shapes.

Enlarged view of the strawberries.

Snail

Thread a strand of double knitting wool through a 150mm (6in) length of tubular ribbon. Sew one end of the ribbon in the middle of the shell shape on the background fabric, then coil the ribbon round this point, ending at the bottom of the shape. Make a bullion knot (see page 29) across the bottom of the shell for the body. Bring knotted lengths of thread up through the head to form the antennae, and trim to size.

Enlarged view of snail.

Butterfly

The wings of the butterfly sitting on one of the cauliflowers are made in the same way as the one on pages 22–25, except that organza is used instead of lightweight calico as the background fabric. The body is a bullion knot.

Full size pattern and exploded view of the elements of the butterfly.

Topiary and pot

The topiary and its pot were made in much the same way as the project design on page 30. However, the trunk is a wrapped length of paper-covered wire, couched to the background fabric.

Fork

The tines of the fork are made from wrapped, paper-covered wire. The handle and shaft are made from a cocktail stick.

Cut two lengths of paper-covered wire – one 40mm (1½in) long, the other 25mm (1in) long – then wrap each length with grey silk. Bend each length into a U shape – one will be slightly smaller than the other, then oversew the two shapes together, one inside the other to form four tines. Trim off any excess wire to equalise the tines.

Cut the points from the cocktail stick, then cut a 12mm (½in) length from one end for the handle. Use wood glue to stick the handle across the shaft and the tines to the bottom of the shaft. Leave to dry for at least twenty-four hours. Paint the handle and shaft with metallic paint, then leave to dry.

Finally, carefully wrap the bottom of the shaft, starting 6mm (¼in) up from the tines. At the bottom, reinforce the join between the tines and the handle with more wrapping. Put it to one side until the man is complete.

Flower bed

Paint pieces of silk fabric in the colours of your choice. When they are completely dry, cut each piece in half and bond together with iron-on interfacing. Cut the silk into 1cm (½in) circles to form the flower heads, then secure each to the background fabric with two or three stab stitches. Add a small bead or French knot in the centre of each flower. Make tufts of leaves in the same way as those for the onions and carrots, then sew these between the flowers. Fill in any gaps with more small beads and/or French knots.

Enlarged view of the flower bed.

Enlarged view of the butterfly.

Gardener

Use the exploded diagram, right, to make the cordonnets and needlelace shape for the clothes, filling each shape with corded single Brussels stitch. Work the hat in two pieces. Top stitch just the bottom edges of the jacket, the arm and the collar of the jacket, then release all the shapes from the backing material.

Cut slightly undersized pieces of felt for the man's legs, his body and his arm, and full size pieces of thin leather for the boots. Sew the felt legs shape to the background fabric, fill it with toy stuffing, then sew the needlelace trousers shape over the felt. Complete the legs by sewing the leather boots over the bottom of the legs. Sew the felt body shape to the background fabric, leaving the bottom edge open. Pad out the top part of this shape with toy stuffing, then secure the bottom with a few loose stab stitches (see page 19).

Now the head must be added. Here, the head is seen from the side, not the front. Make a padded slip as shown on page 72. Draw the head shape on to a piece of lightweight calico, then, starting at the top, back part of the head, sew it to the calico; work clockwise, carefully moulding the padded shape to the drawn outline to ensure you get a good contour, especially round the nose. Referring to the general instruction on pages 69–72, add the eye, mouth, ear and hair. When you are happy with the head shape, work a running stitch 3mm (1/8in) round the outer edge, leaving a loose tail. Cut round the head, 3mm (1/8in) out from the running stitch. Pull up the loose thread to draw the calico behind the head shape, and fasten off. Sew the completed head to the top of the body shape, adding more padding if necessary.

Sew the needlelace sweater to the top of the body shape, ensuring that it covers the bottom of the head. Sew the jacket to the body shape, leaving the bottom edge free. This edge should just extend beyond the edge of the felt. Sew the collar to the top of the jacket.

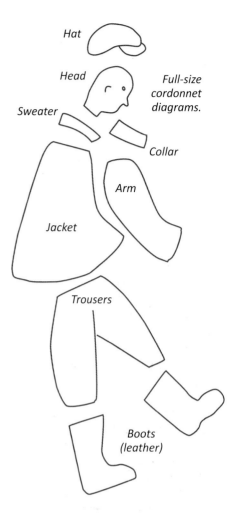

Full-size cordonnet diagrams.

Hat

Head

Sweater

Collar

Arm

Jacket

Trousers

Boots (leather)

Enlarged view of the gardener.

Make one hand (see pages 74–75), leaving at least 25mm (1in) of wire for the arm, then sew the arm on to the background fabric and the body.

Cut a slightly undersize piece of felt for the arm, then sew this over the wired arm and body shape, taking the thread through the background fabric. Cover this with the needlelace arm, leaving the cuff edge free.

Sew the crown of the hat to the top of the head, then sew on its peak, leaving its bottom edge free.

Sew the fork to the background fabric, making two or three couching stitches over the top and bottom ends of the shaft. Mould the man's hand round the handle. Finally, sew the watering-can bead to the background fabric.

The finished embroidery.

Machine-made clothes

For people who prefer machine to hand stitching, machine-made clothes offer a good alternative to needlelace.

Begin by placing a piece of dissolvable fabric into an embroidery hoop and pulling it taut. Pin the paper pattern of the clothes you are making on to the dissolvable fabric, remembering that you will be working with the hoop upside-down so that the fabric lies flat on the bed of the sewing machine. Thread the machine with your chosen thread and outline the shape with straight stitches. Remove the pattern, then fill the shape by sewing lines of stitches backwards and forwards within the outline. Work first in the vertical plane and then in the horizontal. The filling stitches must be worked over the outline stitches otherwise the shape will fall apart when the fabric is dissolved. The more stitches you, the denser the finished texture will be.

When you are satisfied with the stitching, remove the fabric from the embroidery hoop and hold it under running cold water to dissolve the fabric. (It is advisable to put the plug in the sink, otherwise if you drop the piece of machine embroidery it could go down the plug hole!)

The step-by-step pictures below show how you could make the shirt for the fisherman on page 100 using machine stitching.

Fabric clothes may sometimes be more appropriate than needlelace, for example this colourful clown's outfit was made using scraps of material with different patterns on. The fabric you choose should be of the right weight and texture, be easy to sew and manipulate, and any design on it must be in proportion to the picture. To soften a piece of fabric to make it more manageable, try washing it first.

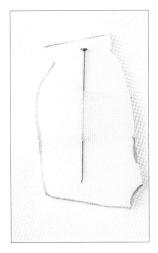

1 Pin the paper pattern to the dissolvable fabric.

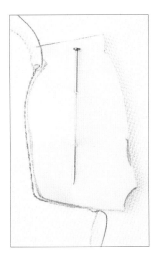

2 Machine stitch around the outside of the pattern.

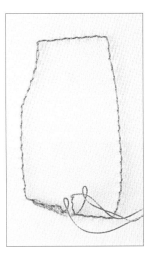

3 When the outline is complete, remove the paper pattern.

4 Fill in the outline using rows of straight stitch, first working vertically and then horizontally.

109

The seasons

The concept of producing an embroidery illustrating the four seasons was originally conceived during discussions at one of Kay's sewing days. One of the ladies present, Neva, sketched out a large circle with pictures showing the four seasons arranged within it; this sketch eventually formed the basis of this embroidery.

Although the original design has evolved considerably, the basic idea is still the same: four pictures, depicting the four seasons, are arranged in a circle, each merging into the next to represent the constant, seamless changing of the seasons throughout the year. The design is based loosely on that of traditional seventeenth-century stumpwork embroideries, in which the various elements were often the same size, so a flower, for example, could be as large as a tree or an animal. As much of the space as possible was filled, and elaborately embroidered, larger-than-life insects were often used to fill in any gaps.

Although the embroidery is designed as a single piece, it is possible to produce four separate embroideries, each depicting a different season.

The finished embroidery, just over half actual size.

110

The first stage in the development of the design was to list everything we wanted to include in each season. We then decided on the background colours. Symmetry and balance are provided by the blue water at the bottom of the picture and the blue winter's sky and snow at the top; and by the greens and browns of spring and autumn on either side. The two trees provide stability and strength, as well as framing the whole picture. Water plays an important part in the overall design; it forms the main component of the summer scene, and blends in to the centre of the picture, drawing everything together. The rocks and grass at the water's edge provide the boundaries between summer, spring and autumn, and the wall and fence form the outer limits of winter.

Once the background elements were in place, we reconsidered what we wanted to include in each season. We decided to put in as many elements as we could without overcrowding, and to use a broad range of colours, textures and techniques, achieving, we hoped, the richness and diversity that typified traditional stumpwork embroideries.

Stitches used in the embroidery

These two pages provide a summary of the more complicated stitches used in the embroidery. Diagrams are provided at the back of the book for easy reference. Although all of the stitches used to create this embroidery are technically correct, some have been adapted for use in stumpwork. For instance, before working long and short stitch, you should place an outline stitch around the shape first to give it a crisp edge. This outline stitch has been omitted from the deer, stag and squirrel to give them a furry appearance.

TIP

Although fine silk is used for some of the stitches on the embroidery, all of them can be worked in six-stranded cotton if you prefer.

Back stitch

Used to outline the autumn tree and the dragonfly's wings. In both cases it is used to support the filling stitches.

Up and down stitch

Used for the grass in the autumn scene.

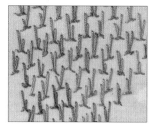 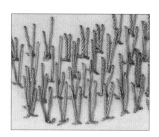

Long and short stitch

A traditional filling stitch, used to make the deer's, stag's and squirrel's fur.

Padded satin stitch

A raised filling stitch, used to make the snowdrop flowers and the dragonfly's body.

Satin stitch

A filling stitch, used for the daffodil petals and the sheep's hooves.

French knots

A versatile stitch, used to make the catkins, the sheep's fleece, the spots on the frog's body, the weeds growing along the bottom of the wall, and the leaves on the autumn tree. Alter the size and texture of the stitch by varying the number of twists you make around the needle and the thickness of the thread.

Fly stitch

Used to make the sheep's eyes and mouths.

Needle-woven picot stitch

Used to make the freestanding daffodil petals and leaves, and the ferns.

Turkey knot stitch

A beautiful textured stitch, used to make the grassy bank, the centre of the lily flower and the squirrel's tail.

Padded raised chain band stitch

A textured filling stitch. It is usually worked in one direction, but here it is worked in two directions to give more texture. Used to fill the trunk of the blossom tree.

Stem stitch

Used to make the daffodil and snowdrop stems, and the snowdrop leaves. Making three or four lines of stitches close together gives the leaves a slightly textured look.

Stab stitch

Used to attach felt padding, slips and other elements to the embroidery.

113

The embroidery

In common with traditional stumpwork, the embroidery is built up in layers, starting with the painted background and finishing with the attachment of raised elements, which are made on separate pieces of fabric, and needlelace.

We begin by showing you how to paint the background fabric, how to transfer the design to the fabric, and how to complete the background embroidery. The project is then divided into four sections – one for each season – which you can either work your way through from beginning to end, or dip into and select the elements you want to work on in whatever order you choose. (Remember, of course, that you need always to work from the back of the embroidery towards the front.) Alternatively, you may wish to adapt the design to produce four smaller, separate embroideries, one for each season.

The embroidery is worked on lightweight calico with a backing of medium-weight calico, secured in a 460mm (18in) embroidery hoop, sometimes known as a quilting hoop. All the stitching will pass through both layers of calico. You will also need a 150mm (6in) hoop, a 255mm (10in) hoop and a 305mm (12in) hoop to make some of the smaller, separate elements. All the materials and equipment you need are listed at the start of each section, and the templates, needlelace patterns and instructions for making the more complicated cordonnets are provided on pages 162–165 and 170–172.

When you are working on your embroidery, make sure your hands are clean and do not put on too much hand cream as this can mark the fabric. Always cover the embroidery with a clean cloth when you are not stitching, and do not place drinks such as tea or coffee near the embroidery in case you accidentally spill them!

The main template

The purpose of the main template is to help you position the various elements on the embroidery. Only the basic outlines are included, as any detail would be covered by the stitching.

You will need to begin by making a full-size copy of the template, shown below. If you have access to a computer scanner, scan in the drawing below and enlarge it two-and-a-half times. Print it out as 'tiles' on to A4 paper and join the pieces together with sticky tape. Alternatively, take it to your local print shop and have it printed on A2 paper, at two-and-a-half times the size shown below. The full-size circle should be 410mm (16¼in) in diameter.

Some useful techniques

There are some techniques that you will use frequently in this project. Mastering these will add to your confidence and greatly improve the quality of your finished embroidery.

Padding

Padding gives depth and texture to stumpwork, and there are various ways of achieving this (see also pages 26 and 28–29). The padding used for the heron (see below), the swan and the wader consists of layered felt; the number of layers you use depends on the effect you wish to achieve. A single layer gives a slightly raised effect, whereas three layers give a domed appearance to the shape. Use a good-quality wool felt and sewing cotton, both in a similar colour to the element you are padding.

Position the first layer of felt over the roundest part of the shape you are padding, pin it in place, and secure it with neat, widely spaced stab stitches. The second layer is slightly larger than the first so that it fits neatly over the top. Use closer stitching to secure this layer. The third layer is a little larger again, and approximately 1mm ($1/16$in) smaller all round than the final shape. Attach it using neat, closely worked stab stitches.

Other types of padding used in stumpwork include interfacing, which gives a raised, hard surface (this has been used for the grass at the bottom of the embroidery), and toy stuffing, used to pad the sheep's heads. Other elements, such as the deer and the stag, are made on a separate piece of fabric, and the excess material is tucked underneath as they are attached to the background to create a padding.

> **TIP**
>
> When attaching a shape to a background using stab stitch, always bring the needle up at an angle from underneath the shape through to the top of the background fabric, and take it back down through the shape. This makes it easier to position the needle, and helps prevent damage to the edge of the shape, particularly when working with felt or leather.

1 Pin the first layer of padding to the lower part of the heron's body and then stab stitch it in place. It should lie approximately 6mm (¼in) inside the gold outline.

2 Attach the second layer over the first in the same way, making sure it fits just within the gold outline. Secure it with six stab stitches spaced evenly around the shape, then fill in the gaps with more stitches.

3 Finally, secure the third and final layer of felt padding so that it sits just on the gold outline. As before, put in a few holding stitches first, then fill in the gaps.

Attaching slips

A slip is a small piece of embroidery that is made separately, and then attached to the main embroidery (see also pages 30–31). The grassy bank, the sheep's bodies, the deer and the stag have all been made on fine calico, while the squirrel's tail has been first embroidered on to organza. Slips should be attached using the same thread with which you made them.

To give a slip a more rounded appearance, cut out the slip and gather the excess material underneath before attaching it to the background fabric, as shown below.

1 Secure the end of the thread, and place running stitches around the outside of the embroidery, approximately 6mm (¼in) from the edge. Leave a long tail thread. Do not secure the thread at this stage.

2 Cut out the slip, just outside the running stitches.

3 Holding the slip firmly, pull the tail thread to gather the fabric. The fabric is then hidden behind the slip. Secure the thread on the back of the fabric.

4 Position the slip on the main embroidery and hold it in position with pins.

5 Use stab stitch to secure the slip in place. Working around the edge of the fabric, put in a few securing stitches first, then fill in the gaps.

The second method of attaching slips is suitable for more intricate shapes, such as the deer, and involves simply tucking the excess fabric underneath the slip as you attach it to the background fabric.

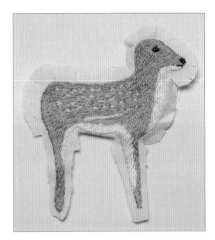  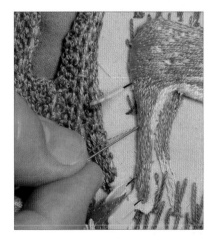

1 Cut out the slip, leaving a 10mm (½in) border around the outside. Snip into the border, cutting in as close as possible to the edge of the slip.

2 Pin the slip in place, tucking the excess fabric underneath. You may find it helpful to use a cocktail stick for this.

3 Stab stitch the slip on to the background, making sure the excess fabric remains neatly tucked underneath as you work.

Needlelace techniques

On the following pages you will learn how to make a needlelace pad, plan the cordonnet for the small lily pad, and work a filling stitch. You will need a No. 9 sharps needle, a No. 9 ballpoint needle and one strand of variegated green six-stranded cotton.

Needlelace pad

Make a sandwich starting with two or three layers of medium-weight calico, followed by the paper pattern, and finally a top protective layer of self-adhesive transparent plastic with the backing removed. Tack all the pieces together firmly. Make the pad large enough to accommodate either a single shape, or several smaller pieces. In the latter case, it is best to complete all the shapes on the pad before releasing any of them.

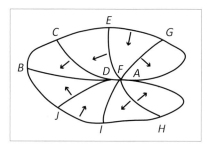

The template for the smallest of the three lily pads (actual size).

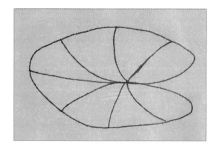

The needlelace pad for the lily pad.

The fish, the swan, the frog, the heron's wing and the lily have all been made using needlelace. Full instructions and patterns are provided later in the book.

Making the cordonnet

It is essential that the cordonnet stays intact when the needlelace is released from the backing fabrics. Take time to plan the layout properly so that you can build the cordonnet from a continuous length of thread. Use the full-size pattern to estimate the length of thread required – lay the thread along the lines on the diagram, double this length of thread and add a small extra allowance. For the small lily pad, you will need 830mm (33in) of thread.

> ## TIP
>
> A poor foundation will result in a disappointing piece of needlelace. Make the couching stitches small, firm and neat, and approximately 3mm (⅛in) apart. Put in an extra stitch on corners and sharp points; the more stitches you put in the less distortion you will get when making the filling stitches. If the couching thread runs out before you have finished the cordonnet, take the thread to the back of the needlelace pad and secure it with three or four stitches, then start a new length.

1 Fold the length of thread in half and lay the looped end over point A, at the end of the main vein. Using a No. 9 sharps needle with a single length of sewing thread, secure the loop with a single stitch worked from inside outwards. Bring the sewing thread back up on the design line, approximately 3mm (⅛in) from A, and make a stitch over the cordonnet threads. Continue couching around the outline until you reach the next leaf vein (point C).

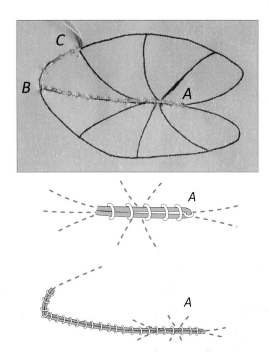

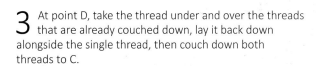

2 At C, separate the cordonnet threads and take one thread down the vein to D, catching it down in one or two places along the design line to hold it in position.

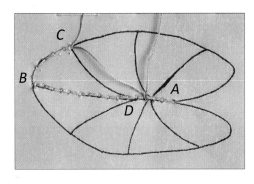

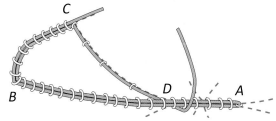

3 At point D, take the thread under and over the threads that are already couched down, lay it back down alongside the single thread, then couch down both threads to C.

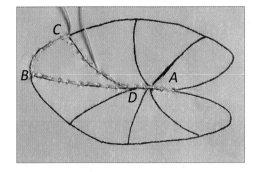

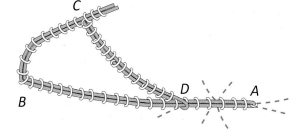

119

4 Continue couching around the outer edge. Make branches at E–F and G–F. As you pass the start loop at A, take one of the threads through the loop, then continue round to H, making branches at H–F, I–F and J–D.

Passing the thread through the start loop, A.

5 After completing the branch J–D, separate the threads and take one thread towards B (see below, left). Take it under and over the cordonnet at B and lay it back towards J, putting in two or three couching stitches to hold it on the design line. Couch down the other thread alongside the existing ones (see below, right), taking it a short distance towards C. Fasten off the couching thread on the back of the pad, then trim away any excess cordonnet threads.

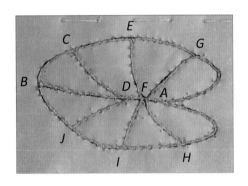

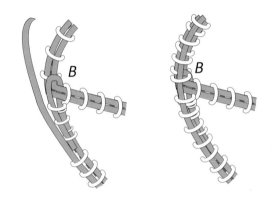

Filling the cordonnet

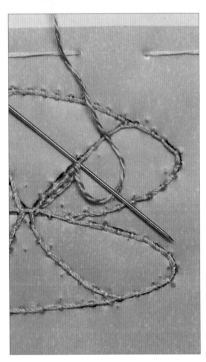

1 Begin to fill one segment of the lily pad with corded single Brussels stitch. Secure the end of the thread to the cordonnet by passing it under a few of the couching stitches, and work a row of evenly spaced buttonhole stitches across the vein. Do not pull the stitches too tight, as in the next row you must work through their loops.

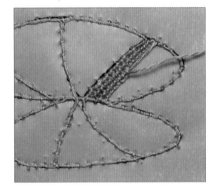

2 When you reach the end of the row, take the needle and thread under then over the two cordonnet threads twice. Lay the thread back across the row as a cord and work back across the shape, working one buttonhole stitch round the cord and through each loop of the previous row. Whip the thread round the cordonnet again and work the next row. Continue working back and forth across the shape until the area is filled. Secure the last row of stitches by whipping each loop to the cordonnet, as shown in the diagram below.

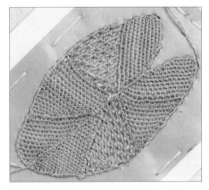

3 Fill each segment of the lily pad. Use double Brussels stitch in two of the segments; double Brussels stitch is a more open, lacy stitch that breaks up the solidity of the corded single Brussels stitch.

Whipping a thread to the cordonnet.

Finishing

Needlelace is traditionally finished with a raised outer edge. This is achieved by top stitching. Only edges that are freestanding, such as the bottom edge of the swan's wing, require top stitching; other edges are stab stitched to the background fabric. Top stitching can also be used to highlight a surface detail, such as the veins on the lily pad. Once the top stitching is complete, remove the needlelace from the pad.

TIP

Fine wire can be added under the top stitching, allowing the edge to be sculpted.

1 Using the same thread as the filling stitches, lay two threads along the veins of the lily pad, and attach them using closely worked buttonhole stitches.

2 Complete the top stitching along each of the veins, and around the outer edge of the lily pad.

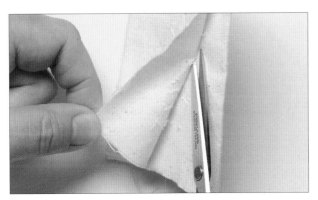

3 Remove the tacking stitches around the outside of the pad, fold apart the last two layers of calico, then use fine-pointed scissors to snip through the stitches.

4 Remove the needlelace, and use tweezers to remove any remaining couching threads.

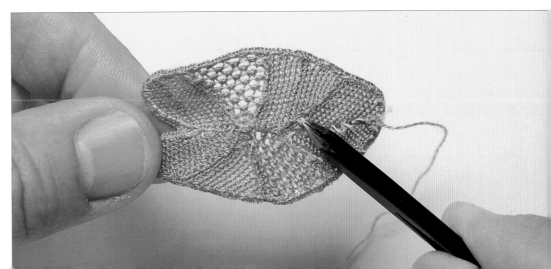

Getting started

In this section you will learn how to prepare the background for your embroidery, before adding the main elements. If you intend to produce a smaller embroidery, based on one of the four seasons, you will need to adapt the quantities and sizes of materials as appropriate. You will need a large, flat surface to work on, in a well-lit area, and a comfortable chair. If you prefer to use a stand, you may need two to provide adequate support for the embroidery.

Painting the background

Watersoluble crayons are used to colour the background fabric. Use horizontal strokes and the flat side of the 'point' of the crayon to lay the colour on to the calico. When using two or three colours, lay the colour in the spaces that are left rather than on top of previous colours, then mix them after all the colours are in place.

1 Lay the lightweight calico on a hard, flat surface. Start painting by lightly marking in the edge of the winter sky using a mid-blue watersoluble crayon. Place the embroidery hoop over the fabric as a guide.

2 Remove the hoop and colour in the sky using light, horizontal strokes. Leave two patches only lightly covered so they can be filled with a second colour.

3 Lightly fill one patch with grey and the other with red.

4 Secure the calico in the hoop to raise it off the surface, and dampen the sky using clean water applied with a large paintbrush. Use just enough water to ensure the colours blend.

Materials

- 460mm (18in) embroidery hoop, with a bound inner ring
- 150mm (6in) embroidery hoop
- Silk frame, 380mm (15in) square, and pins
- Large pair of embroidery scissors
- No. 9 embroidery needle, No. 9 sharps needle, No. 9 ballpoint needle and a darning needle
- Lace pins and berry-head pins
- Main template (full size)
- Full-size templates for the water and grass
- Needlelace pad(s) for the freestanding snowdrop petals and dragonfly wings
- Medium-weight calico, 610mm (24in) square
- Lightweight calico, 610mm (24in) square
- Silk organza, 410mm (16¼in) square
- Silk chiffon, 410mm (16¼in) square
- Silk noil, 410mm (16¼in) square
- Heavy-weight interfacing,
- 355 x 130mm (14 x 5in)
- Six-stranded cotton in yellow and various shades of green
- Variegated six-stranded cotton in grey-blue and green
- Variegated stranded silk in brown-green
- 100/3 fine silk thread in white
- Variegated metallic thread
- Bullion thread in silver-blue
- Sewing cotton
- Fine copper wire
- Blue-coloured fine copper wire
- Watersoluble crayons in mid-blue, grey, red, dark green and light green
- Fabric paints in blue and light green
- Three or four paintbrushes in a range of sizes
- Absorbent paper
- Gold gel pen
- Lightbox (optional)
- PVA glue

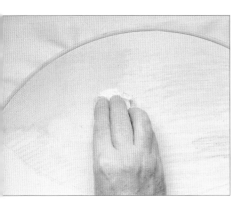

5 Dab out any excess colour (where it looks too dark) using a piece of absorbent paper.

6 Once the winter background has dried, colour the other three seasons in the same way. Paint the backgrounds for autumn and spring using dark green and light green respectively, and paint the area in the centre of the fabric blue.

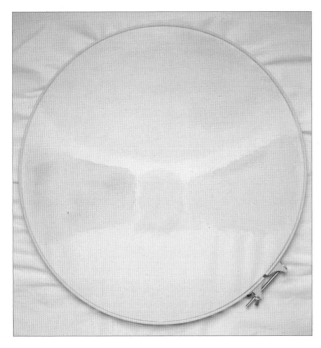

TIP

When painting the background, do not add water while the calico is resting on a hard surface, as the fabric will not dry and the paint will spread.

7 Adjust the colours by strengthening them where necessary using the watersoluble crayons, or softening them by dabbing with a paper towel. Allow the paint to dry.

Transferring the design

Remove the calico from the hoop and centre it over the main template. You may wish to pin the two together to avoid the fabric slipping. Work either over a lightbox or by a sunny window so that the design shows clearly through the fabric. Using a gold gel pen, carefully trace over the outlines on the paper template.

Place the painted calico with the gold outlines on top of the piece of medium-weight calico, and mount the two layers of fabric in the hoop ready to begin the embroidery.

The background embroidery

Embroider the trunk of the blossom tree, the petals, stems and leaves of the daffodils on the right-hand side of the picture (the trumpets, and more freestanding daffodils, will be added later), the snowdrop and the dragonfly in the centre, and the grass on the left.

Daffodils

Begin by working the stems in stem stitch, following the lines transferred on to the background fabric. Use a No. 9 embroidery needle threaded with two strands of light green six-stranded cotton. Work the three petals of each flower that are drawn on to the background in satin stitch using one strand of yellow cotton. The other three petals are needle-woven picots, see page 174, approximately 6mm (¼in) long, worked using a ballpoint needle directly on to the background fabric, and placed between the existing petals. The leaves are also needle-woven picots, worked straight on to the background using a single strand of light green six-stranded cotton, and varying in length up to approximately 20mm (¾in).

Grass

Randomly work three areas of grass (refer to the photograph on page 124). It does not matter if some grass is later covered by the deer, tree or rocks. Use up and down stitch, in various lengths, worked with two strands of variegated green six-stranded cotton and an embroidery needle.

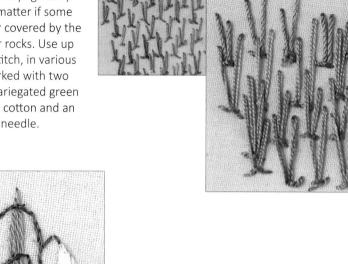

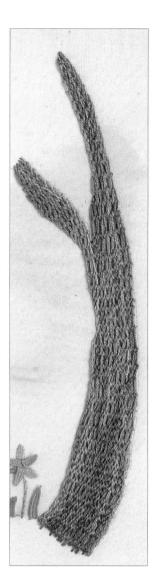

Snowdrop

Work the leaves as four rows of stem stitch, worked closely together, using an embroidery needle and one strand of mid-green six-stranded cotton. Next work the stems as a single row of stem stitch using a darker green thread. The petals are padded satin stitch worked with one strand of white 100/3 fine silk and an embroidery needle.

Tree trunk

The trunk of the blossom tree is worked in padded raised chain band stitch, see page 175. Work up and down the length of the tree for added texture, using two strands of variegated brown-green stranded silk and an embroidery needle.

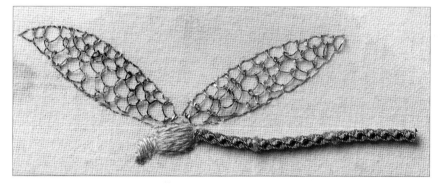

Dragonfly

Use padded satin stitch for the body and head, worked with one strand of variegated grey-blue six-stranded cotton and an embroidery needle. Outline the two wings in back stitch using variegated metallic thread, and fill them with single Brussels stitch using the back stitch instead of a cordonnet for support. Cut a 30mm (1¼in) length of silver-blue bullion thread. Thread a ballpoint needle with one strand of variegated grey-blue six-stranded cotton, bring it through to the front of the fabric and pass it along the core of the bullion thread. Take it back through to the back of the fabric, then return it to the front of the work and secure the bullion thread with one or two couching stitches.

The water

For the water, use a piece of blue-painted organza overlaid with blue-painted chiffon.

  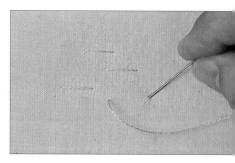

1 Attach the piece of silk organza to a 380 x 380mm (15 x 15in) silk frame. Using a large brush, wet the fabric first then apply a watery mix of blue fabric paint. Leave the paint to dry. Paint the silk chiffon in the same way.

2 Using the template on page 169, cut the shape of the water from each piece of silk. Position the organza on the background fabric at the bottom of the picture, overlay it with the chiffon and pin both pieces of fabric in place.

3 Stab stitch both layers to the background fabric, placing stitches only where they will eventually be covered by rocks or grass so they won't be visible on the finished embroidery. Create the ripples by placing single straight stitches randomly over the central part of the water. Use a single strand of grey-blue six-stranded cotton.

The grass

For the grass at the bottom of the embroidery, cut a piece of interfacing using the template supplied on page 169 and paint it with light green fabric paint. Paint an area of silk noil that is slightly larger than the template using the same colour. Allow both to dry.

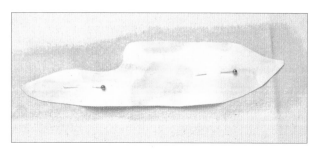

1 Pin the interfacing face down to the wrong side of the green-painted noil using berry-head pins.

2 Cut around the interfacing, leaving a 20mm (¾in) border.

3 Make snips in the border, cutting up to the edge of the interfacing, fold over the tabs and stick them down using PVA glue.

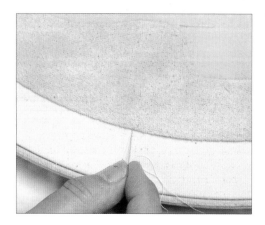

4 Attach the grass to the background fabric using stab stitches.

Completing the snowdrop and dragonfly

The snowdrop and dragonfly, which lie in the centre of the embroidery, can now be completed. Alternatively, you may prefer to do this later, incorporating them into one of the seasons, as both elements are made of needlelace and are very fragile; attach the dragonfly's wings as the last stage of summer, and the needlelace snowdrop petals at the end of spring. The patterns for these are provided on pages 162 and 163.

Snowdrop

The freestanding snowdrop petals are very delicate, and care must be taken when attaching them to the background fabric. They are made in needlelace, using one strand of 100/3 fine silk. Couch a fine wire around the outside with the cordonnet, and fill the shape using corded single Brussels stitch.

Attach the completed petals by making a small hole in the fabric at the top of the lower left-hand stem with a darning needle, and passing the wires through to the back of the work. Bend the wires so they lie along the back of the flower. Take the tail threads from the needlelace through to the back of the fabric and use them to overstitch the wires in place.

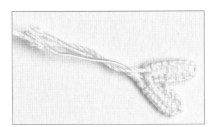

The completed freestanding petals.

Dragonfly

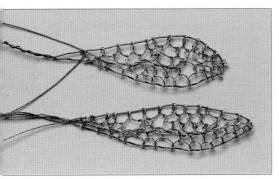

1 Begin by couching a thin, blue-coloured copper wire around the outside of each wing to stiffen it, working from the base of the wing, around the tip, and back to the base. Twist the two ends of the wire together. Using the variegated metallic thread, work buttonhole stitches around the inside of each wing, again starting at the base and working round the tip (see diagram below). Repeat once more, working the buttonhole stitches into the loops of the previous row. Work one more row from the base of the wing to the tip, then whip the thread through each buttonhole-stitch loop back to the base.

The filling stitches for the dragonfly's wings.

2 To attach the needlelace wings, make two adjacent holes in the embroidery, just below the existing wings, using a darning needle, and pass the wires and threads through to the back of the fabric. Use the threads to secure the wings by overstitching the wires in place. Lift and shape the wings so they stand proud of the background.

127

Winter

The winter scene is possibly the easiest of the four seasons to make, and as it is at the top of the embroidery it seems logical to make it first.

We chose a snow scene, set against the painted winter sky, with a log cabin and two fir trees. The snow is carded cotton that has been teased out and held in place by stab stitches. The fir trees are made in needlelace. To represent snow resting on their boughs, the small tree is edged with top stitching using a white, fine silk thread, and the large tree is edged with white bouclé wool. Attach the smaller tree first, and then the snow. Next attach the larger tree, and finally add the log cabin, making sure the snow overlaps its base.

The needlelace patterns for the fir trees, and instructions for making the smaller tree's cordonnet, are provided on page 162. The template for the log cabin (given on page 172) includes cutting lines for the windows and door, and should be photocopied on to an A4 sheet of paper.

Materials

- Embroidery, general-purpose and large scissors
- No. 9 embroidery needle, No. 9 sharps needle and No. 9 ballpoint needle
- Lace pins
- Full-size template for the padding for the large fir tree's trunk
- Full-size template for the log cabin, copied on to A4 paper
- Needlelace pad(s) for the two fir trees
- Silk organza, 150mm (6in) square
- Small piece of dark brown felt
- 2mm (⅛in)-thick lime wood planking, 5 x 915mm (¼ x 36in)
- 2mm (⅛in)-thick balsa wood, 75 x 305mm (3 x 12in)
- Small quantity of toy stuffing
- Cotton fibres
- Six-stranded cotton in dark green, brown and white
- 100/3 fine silk thread in dark green and white
- Silver metallic sewing thread
- Sewing cotton
- White bouclé wool
- Watersoluble crayons in mid-brown, red and white
- Small paintbrush
- PVA glue
- Cutting mat
- Heavy-duty craft knife
- Small craft knife
- Nail file
- Steel ruler
- Cocktail stick
- Tweezers
- Damp sponge

The fir trees and snow

Both the fir trees are made in needlelace using corded single Brussels stitch.

The small tree

The small tree is made in one piece, with the cordonnet running around the outside of each section of foliage (see page 162). It is made using a single strand of dark green six-stranded cotton, with white 100/3 silk used for the top stitching along the edges of the foliage. After releasing the needlelace from its pad, take all the loose threads through to the back of the work and use these to stab stitch the tree on to the background fabric.

The snow

Tease out a clump of cotton fibres, enough to lay all the snow in one go, and arrange it on the background. Make sure it covers the base of the small fir tree. Place stab stitches, worked with a single strand of white six-stranded cotton, randomly over the snow to hold it in place.

The large tree

The large tree is made in four separate parts, with a trunk that is applied over a layer of felt padding to give it a rounded appearance. Use the same dark green thread as you used for the small tree, and brown for the trunk.

1 Edge each section of the tree in white bouclé wool to resemble snow, couched down using silver metallic sewing thread to give a hint of sparkle to the tree.

2 Cut out the felt padding for the trunk using the template on page 170 and stab stitch it in place. Pin then sew the trunk over the felt padding. Pin the lower section of the foliage in place and secure it with stab stitches along the two sides and the top edge. Use a silver metallic thread.

3 Attach the other three sections of the tree in the same way. At the top of the tree, take any tail threads through to the back of the fabric and secure them.

Log cabin

The logs for the cabin are made from lime wood, which is traditionally used for making model boats. All the logs are tapered to give a more realistic finish. You will construct the cabin on the template, placed on a cutting mat (don't worry if the paper sticks to the back of the cabin – it will help bind the model together). Keep a damp sponge to hand to remove any excess glue before it dries.

A simplified version can be made by replacing the sides of the cabin with balsa wood and painting in the details.

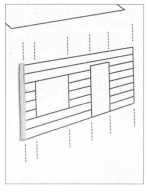

1 Starting with the front of the cabin, cut the left-hand corner piece from a strip of 2mm (¹⁄₁₆in)-thick lime wood. Round off the sides on one face using a nail file, cut it to the right length and place it on the template.

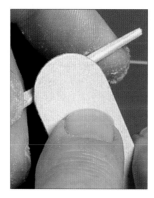

2 Cut eight 40mm (1½in) lengths of lime wood. Taper them using a nail file (or a small craft knife and steel ruler), and round off the corners on one face.

3 Dip the widest end of one of the logs in PVA glue, lie it along the top edge of the wall, and push it firmly against the corner piece to secure it. Apply glue to the rest of the logs and position them in the same way. Let the glue dry and trim them to the right length.

4 Aligning your ruler with the vertical guide lines, cut out the window and door with the heavy-duty craft knife.

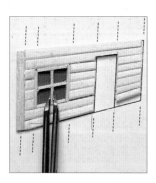

5 Cut the paper away from the window. To make the window frame, use thin strips of balsa wood – cut to approximately 0.5mm (¹⁄₃₂in) thick and 1mm (¹⁄₁₆in) wide – apply PVA glue to them using a cocktail stick and manoeuvre them into position with tweezers.

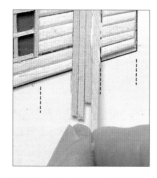

6 For the door, cut approximately four strips of 1 x 1mm (¹⁄₁₆in) balsa wood, slightly longer than the height of the doorway. Run glue down one side of each strip and slot them in place one at a time.

7 Trim off the excess wood at the bottom of the door with a craft knife.

8 For the side of the cabin you will need 16 tapered strips of lime wood, each 50mm (2in) long. Make it in one piece, attaching the logs following the same method you used for the front of the cabin. Cut out the windows and chimney following the guide lines. Attach the left corner post and, using a strip of balsa wood, the eave behind the chimney. Cut the paper away from the windows and fit the frames.

9 For the chimney, cut a 45 x 10mm (1¾ x ½in) piece of balsa wood, which is a little longer than it needs to be, and attach a narrow 2 x 2mm (¹⁄₁₆ x ¹⁄₁₆in) strip to each side.

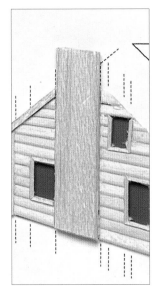

10 Apply glue along the two thin strips and secure the chimney in position.

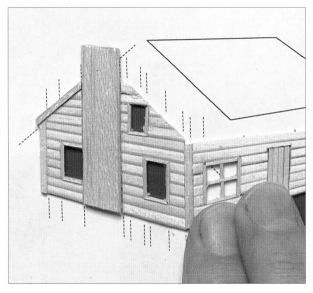

11 Cut out the front of the cabin using a small craft knife and glue it to the side.

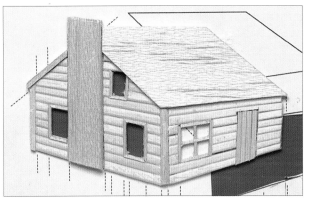

12 Cut out the first layer of the roof from 2mm (¹⁄₁₆in)-thick balsa wood using the template. Cut the second layer so that it is 2mm (¹⁄₁₆in) deeper and wider, and glue it on top of the first. Cut off the top left-hand corner to fit round the chimney. Make sure the roof fits neatly and cut away any excess wood with the large craft knife. Glue it in place using PVA glue.

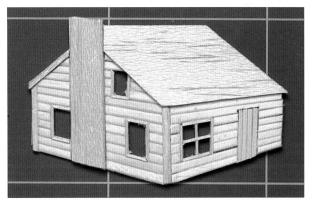

13 Cut the completed cabin away from the paper.

14 To complete the cabin, use watersoluble crayons to paint the logs brown and the chimney red, adding white lines to the chimney when the paint is dry to suggest brickwork. Glue a layer of organza behind the windows, and attach the cabin to the background using PVA glue. Make sure the snow overlaps the base of the cabin. Place a thin layer of cotton fibres on the roof, not forgetting the eave behind the chimney, stick it down with PVA glue, and push a small amount of toy stuffing into the chimney for smoke.

Spring

For this part of the embroidery, we have chosen elements traditionally associated with spring – grazing sheep and lambs, framed by golden daffodils, catkins and blossom. Here we introduce slips in the form of the sheep and lambs and the clumps of grass. Gloving leather has been used for the sheep's faces and French knots for their fleece; the grass consists of turkey knot stitch.

The catkin boughs and the blossom boughs (there are two of each) are constructed separately before being attached to the background, the rocks are made from pressed-paper egg boxes, and the fence from balsa wood.

Additional freestanding daffodils are added to the scene, and trumpets added to those already embroidered on to the background. All these elements together add texture and depth, which are enhanced by the use of variegated threads to make the tree trunk, the grass and the ferns.

Materials

- 150mm (6in) embroidery hoop
- Embroidery, general-purpose and large scissors
- Nos. 7 and 9 embroidery needles, No. 9 sharps needle, No. 9 ballpoint needle and a darning needle
- Lace pins and berry-head pins
- Full-size templates for the clumps of grass and the sheep
- Full-size template for the fence, copied on to A4 paper
- Needlelace pad(s) for the blossom petals, and blossom and catkin leaves
- Five pieces of lightweight calico, each 205mm (8in) square
- Silk organza, 205mm (8in) square
- Cream gloving leather, 130 x 75mm (5 x 3in)
- 4mm (1/8in)-thick balsa wood, 75 x 305mm (3 x 12in)
- Watersoluble fabric, 205mm (8in) square
- Toy stuffing
- Six-stranded cotton in cream, yellow, green, dark brown and light brown
- Variegated six-stranded cotton in greens, yellows, browns, reds and pinks
- 100/3 fine silk thread in yellow, green and pink
- Silk noil thread in green
- Sewing cotton
- Fine tapestry wool in cream
- Fine copper wire
- Paper-covered wire
- Watersoluble crayons in brown and green
- Medium-sized paintbrush
- Gold gel pen
- PVA glue
- Cocktail stick
- Tweezers
- Heavy-duty craft knife
- Small craft knife
- Cutting mat
- Pressed-paper egg boxes
- Transparent sticky tape
- Metal ruler
- Damp sponge

Grassy bank

Many of the elements in this section have been made as slips before being attached to the background fabric. Start with the grass itself, which should be worked as four, progressively smaller, slips. Begin by securing a piece of lightweight calico in a small embroidery hoop, then work all four slips together before cutting them out and attaching them to the background fabric. The templates for the clumps of grass are provided on page 171.

Grass

1   Create the largest of the four clumps of grass by working twelve rows of turkey knot stitch using three strands of variegated green six-stranded cotton and a No. 9 embroidery needle. For the remaining three slips, work successively fewer rows.

2   Cut out the slips and gather the excess fabric underneath (see page 117). Cut through the ends of the loops of the turkey knot stitches using a pair of sharp scissors.

A completed clump of grass.

3   Pin the largest clump of grass to the background, at the base of the tree, and stab stitch it in place.

4   Attach the second clump alongside, to the left, followed by the remaining two, ending with the smallest clump.

Ferns

These are made separately on a piece of silk organza secured in a 150mm (6in) embroidery hoop. This fabric works well as a base for slips, as it is fine, easy to cut out, and virtually invisible when attached to the background fabric. Each fern is made up of four to six fronds, each approximately 16–18mm (¾in) long, worked in a tight circle, with the bases of the fronds overlapping.

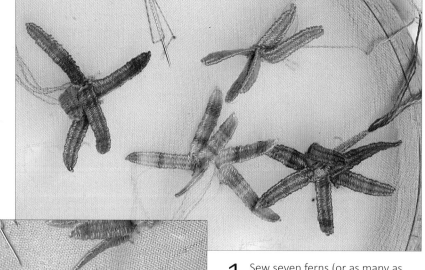

1 Sew seven ferns (or as many as you like) on to the organza using needle-woven picot stitch, see page 174. Use one strand of variegated six-stranded cotton in various shades of yellow, green, brown and red. Leave long tail threads with which to attach each fern to your embroidery.

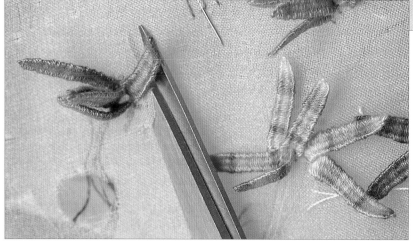

2 Carefully cut out each fern, leaving a circle of organza around the base.

TIP

You may wish to make extra ferns and rocks (page 136) to use in the summer scene (see page 150).

3 Position each of the ferns on your embroidery, take the tail threads through to the back of the fabric and secure them.

Daffodils

You will need to make three or four freestanding daffodils, and enough trumpets for all of the flowers, including those embroidered on to the background (see page 124). The freestanding daffodil petals are made with 100/3 fine silk on a small piece of watersoluble fabric secured in a small embroidery hoop. Each flower head consists of five needle-woven picots, each approximately 5mm (¼in) long, worked in a tight circle.

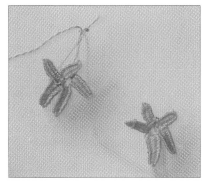

1 Make three or four groups of daffodil petals using needle-woven picot stitch, see page 174. Use a single strand of 100/3 fine silk, in the same shade of yellow as the background daffodils.

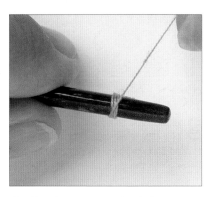

2 For the trumpets, begin by threading a needle with a single strand of yellow six-stranded cotton, and wind it three times around the end of a paintbrush.

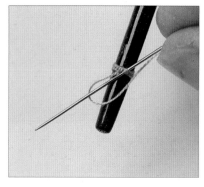

3 Work one row of buttonhole stitch around the circle of threads.

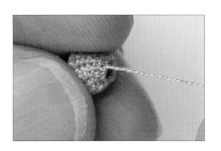

4 Work a further five rows of buttonhole stitch. Weave the thread through the last row of stitches, slip the stitching off the end of the paintbrush, and pull the thread tight to form a cup shape.

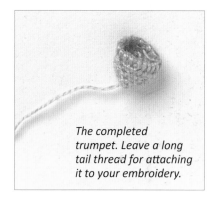

The completed trumpet. Leave a long tail thread for attaching it to your embroidery.

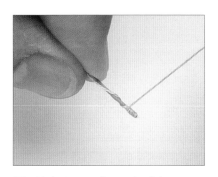

5 Make a stem for each of the freestanding daffodils. Take an 80mm (3¼in) length of paper-covered wire, dip the end in PVA glue and closely wrap a single strand of green six-stranded cotton around the first 6mm (¼in).

6 Cut out a ring of petals and dampen the watersoluble fabric to dissolve it away. Push the tip of a stem up through the centre of the flower. Make sure the green thread remains at the back so that you can use it to wrap round the rest of the stem.

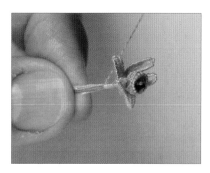

7 Slip the trumpet over the tip of the wire and pass the thread through to the back of the flower. Continue wrapping the green thread around the wire and all the loose threads to form the stem. It should be approximately 20mm (¾in) long. Secure the green thread at the end with either a knot or a dab of PVA glue, leaving a long tail.

A completed daffodil.

8 Attach the freestanding daffodils to the background by slipping the ends of the stems behind the grass and oversewing them in place using the green thread. Attach the trumpets to the background flowers by passing the threads through to the back of the fabric and securing them.

Rocks

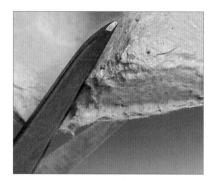

1 Cut out the shapes for the rocks from pressed-paper egg boxes.

2 Colour each rock using green and brown watersoluble crayons.

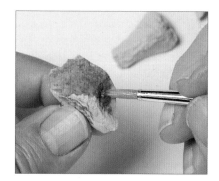

3 Apply water with a damp paintbrush to blend the colours.

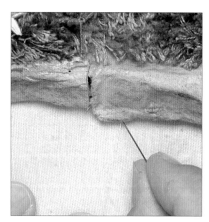

4 Attach the rocks to the background by pushing them up underneath the grass a little way and stab stitching them in place.

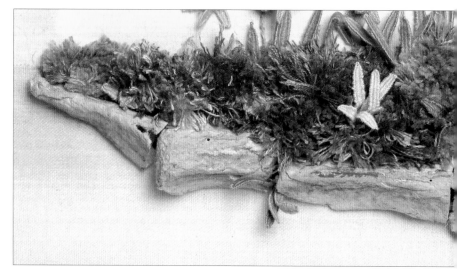

5 To finish, push a clump of ferns (see page 134) into one of the crevices between the rocks, pass the thread through, pull it taut and secure it at the back of your work.

Fence

The fence is made of balsa wood, which is a soft wood that is easy to cut using a good, strong craft knife with a sharp blade. You will need a copy of the template on A4 paper, covered with transparent sticky tape. This will prevent the balsa wood from sticking to the paper when you glue the parts together. Work on a cutting mat, and use a damp sponge to wipe away any excess glue before it dries.

1 Begin by cutting a 4mm (⅛in) wide strip from the balsa wood using a heavy-duty craft knife and a metal ruler.

2 Lay it over the first fence post on the template and trim it to the correct length.

3 Give the wood a distressed look by randomly trimming thin slivers from the corners using a small craft knife. Always cut away from you.

4 Place the fence post on the template and cut three 4mm (⅛in) wide pieces of wood for the first three rails, making them slightly longer than required. Give each of them a distressed finish, and trim the left-hand end off at a slight angle.

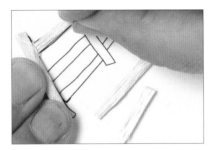

5 Dip the left-hand end of each rail in PVA glue and position the rails on the template, pushing them firmly against the first post.

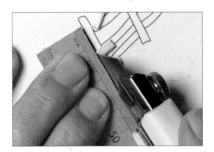

6 Trim the rails to the correct length by laying a ruler across them and cutting with the heavy-duty craft knife.

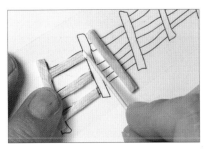

7 Make the next fence post, and apply glue to the right-hand ends of the rails using a cocktail stick to secure it.

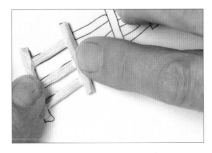

8 Fix the second post in place.

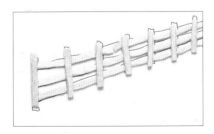

9 Complete the remainder of the fence in the same way. When all the glue has dried, scrape off the excess with the small craft knife.

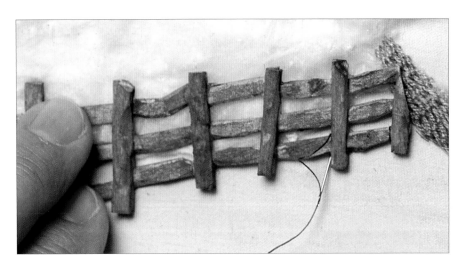

10 Paint the fence using brown watersoluble crayon, allow it to dry and position it on your embroidery so that the lower edge of the bottom rails aligns with the gold line drawn on the background fabric, and the left-hand end is just to the right of the snowdrop. If necessary, trim the right-hand end of the fence so that it sits neatly against the tree trunk. Sew the fence in place by taking a stitch over each of the bottom rails, next to the fence posts.

Blossom

Each leaf and petal of the blossom bough is made individually in needlelace, the patterns for which are provided on page 163. You can make as many flowers and leaves as you like – in this example there are four large flowers, each with five petals; five medium-sized flowers with four petals each; four small flowers, also with four petals; twelve small leaves; and five large leaves. In addition, you will need three large leaves to hide the points at which you attach the boughs to the embroidery. The instructions below are for a single blossom bough; you will need to make two altogether.

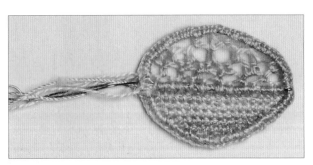

Make each leaf using variegated green six-stranded cotton. Couch a thin copper wire around the outside with the cordonnet, and along the central vein (see page 163). Fill one half of the shape using corded single Brussels stitch, and the other half using double Brussels stitch (see page 45). Leave tail threads of approximately 50mm (2in), and apply top stitching around the outside.

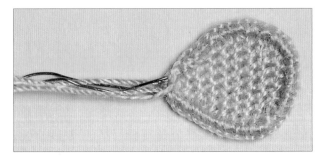

Make each petal using variegated pink six-stranded cotton. Couch a thin copper wire around the outside with the cordonnet, and fill the shape using corded single Brussels stitch. Leave tail threads of approximately 50mm (2in), and apply top stitching to the outside.

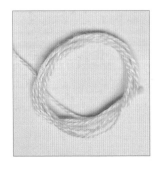

1 Make the stamens in the centre of each flower by first wrapping a 250mm (10in) length of cream six-stranded cotton around your forefinger to create several loops.

2 For the large flowers, group three petals together, right-side up, as shown in the photograph, and place the looped yellow thread on top of them. For the smaller flowers, use only two petals.

3 Lay two more petals on top, face down, and bind all the tail threads and wires together by wrapping a single green cotton thread around them to form the stems. Wind the thread down for approximately 10mm (½in), leaving the rest of the stem bare.

4 Arrange the petals to form the shape of the flower, and snip through the ends of the loops to make the stamens.

5 To form the blossom bough, work from the top of the bough downwards. Bind the top two flowers together first, then gradually bind in the other elements. Use the tail threads for binding, knotting them at the end to secure them. It does not matter in what order you combine the elements.

The completed blossom bough.

Catkins

The two catkin boughs are made in a similar way to the blossom boughs. In this example there are five catkins and five leaves for each one, though again you can make as many elements as you wish.

The catkins are made as freestanding elements, for which you will need two layers of lightweight calico supported in a small embroidery hoop. The leaves are needlelace, made in the same way as the blossom leaves, using the pattern for the small leaves on page 163.

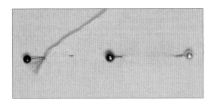

1 To make the catkins, insert three berry-head pins into the calico, 25mm (1in) apart, as shown above. Tie a 305mm (12in) length of cream six-stranded cotton around the left-hand pin.

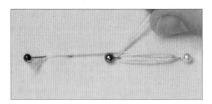

2 Take the cotton around the right-hand pin and wind it around this and the middle pin three times.

3 Separate off one strand of thread using the eye end of a No. 7 embroidery needle.

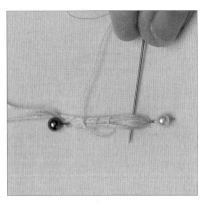

4 Thread the single strand through the needle and use it to bind together the wound threads.

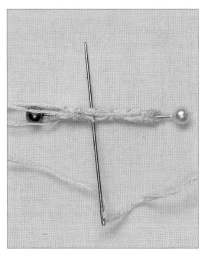

5 Separate off another two strands, thread them through the needle and work French knots over the surface of the bound threads.

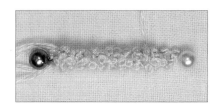

A completed catkin.

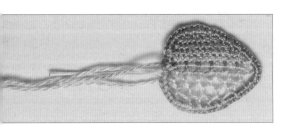

Make each leaf using a variegated green thread following the same method used for the small leaves on the blossom boughs (see page 163).

6 Begin to make the bough by dipping the end of a 100mm (4in) length of paper-covered wire in PVA glue. Wrap the first 10mm (½in) in green silk noil, then bind in the first catkin.

7 Continue down the branch for approximately 30mm (1¼in), binding in another catkin and a leaf. Work two other branches in the same way, one with two catkins and two leaves and the other with one catkin and one leaf. Bind in these other two branches, following the picture left, together with another single leaf, to create the bough.

Attaching the blossom and catkins

1 Attach each blossom bough to the embroidery. For each one, make a hole at the top of the tree using a darning needle, insert the end of the blossom in the hole, and secure it at the back of your work by overstitching.

2 Attach the catkin boughs, just below the blossom boughs, using the same method. Attach three large leaves to cover the places where the boughs pass through the embroidery. Attach the leaves by passing the stems through to the back and securing them with overstitching.

Sheep

The sheep heads are made out of soft gloving leather, and the bodies are made using French knots. The fleece is worked in tapestry wool for a soft, woolly appearance; for the lambs' fleece we used two strands of six-stranded cotton. Make the bodies as separate slips on a piece of lightweight calico mounted in a small embroidery hoop. All the bodies can be made at the same time, on the same piece of calico. Similarly, all the heads can be made together, on another piece of fine calico.

When working with leather, always use a new, fine sharps needle, and avoid making unnecessary holes in the material.

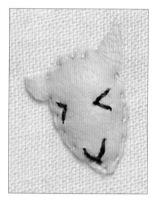

TIP

If the sheep is looking down, use ℧ shapes for the eyes; to make them look straight forward, turn the ℧s on their sides, as shown left.

1 Cut out all the head shapes using the templates provided on page 172 and stab stitch them to the calico using a strand of six-stranded cotton. Sew from the chin up to one ear, then from the chin to the other ear. Place a single stitch just above each ear and leave the top of the head open. Do not stitch the ears down.

2 Stuff the head using toy stuffing. Push it in using the end of a cocktail stick.

3 Sew up the head and embroider the eyes and mouth using a single strand of dark brown six-stranded cotton. Use two straight stitches for each eye and a fly stitch for the mouth.

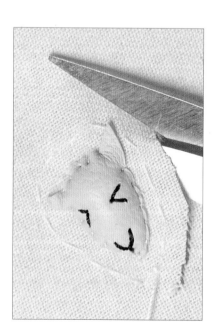

4 Sew around the outside of the head using running stitch, leaving a 3mm (⅛in) gap, then cut around the slip approximately 3mm (⅛in) from the stitching.

5 Pull the running stitch tight so that the surplus calico goes up behind the head.

142

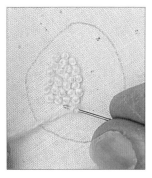

6 For the sheep's bodies, draw the outlines on to calico with a gold gel pen using the templates provided, and fill them with closely worked French knots. Use a No. 7 embroidery needle and two strands of cream six-stranded cotton for the lambs' fleece and one strand of tapestry wool, as shown above, for the adults.

7 Make the slips for the sheep's bodies in the same way as the heads (see steps 4 and 5).

A completed lamb's body.

8 Make each of the ram's horns by dipping the end of a 30mm (1¼in) length of paper-covered wire in PVA glue and wrapping it tightly with light brown six-stranded cotton.

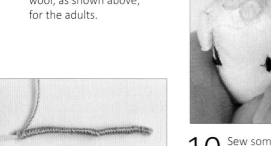

9 Bind approximately 20mm (¾in) of the wire, leaving 10mm (½in) bare. Knot the end of the thread, leaving a long tail with which to attach the horn to the ram's head.

10 Sew some French knots on top of the ram's head using the tapestry wool. Make a small hole just behind the ear. Bend the wire into a coil, dip the bare end in PVA glue and insert it into the hole. Attach the second horn in the same way.

11 Position the sheep's bodies on the background fabric and stab stitch them in place. Attach the sheep's heads, making sure they sit on top of the bodies and are not separate from them.

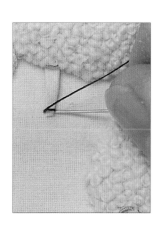

12 Cut out the sheep's legs from a piece of leather using the templates provided on page 172. Tuck them under the body and secure them with two small holding stitches. Sew on the hooves using satin stitch worked in a single strand of dark brown six-stranded cotton.

The completed sheep. Add some long stitches and French knots, using a single strand of green six-stranded cotton, to resemble grass.

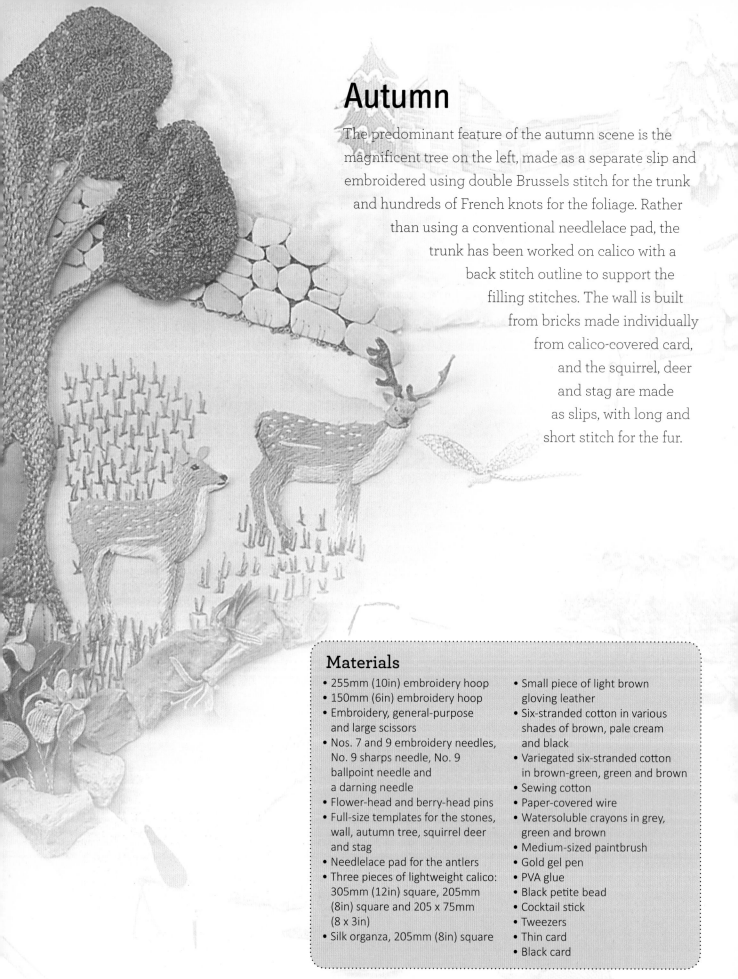

Autumn

The predominant feature of the autumn scene is the magnificent tree on the left, made as a separate slip and embroidered using double Brussels stitch for the trunk and hundreds of French knots for the foliage. Rather than using a conventional needlelace pad, the trunk has been worked on calico with a back stitch outline to support the filling stitches. The wall is built from bricks made individually from calico-covered card, and the squirrel, deer and stag are made as slips, with long and short stitch for the fur.

Materials

- 255mm (10in) embroidery hoop
- 150mm (6in) embroidery hoop
- Embroidery, general-purpose and large scissors
- Nos. 7 and 9 embroidery needles, No. 9 sharps needle, No. 9 ballpoint needle and a darning needle
- Flower-head and berry-head pins
- Full-size templates for the stones, wall, autumn tree, squirrel deer and stag
- Needlelace pad for the antlers
- Three pieces of lightweight calico: 305mm (12in) square, 205mm (8in) square and 205 x 75mm (8 x 3in)
- Silk organza, 205mm (8in) square

- Small piece of light brown gloving leather
- Six-stranded cotton in various shades of brown, pale cream and black
- Variegated six-stranded cotton in brown-green, green and brown
- Sewing cotton
- Paper-covered wire
- Watersoluble crayons in grey, green and brown
- Medium-sized paintbrush
- Gold gel pen
- PVA glue
- Black petite bead
- Cocktail stick
- Tweezers
- Thin card
- Black card

Wall

The first step is to paint a piece of lightweight calico measuring 205 x 75mm (8 x 3in), using watersoluble crayons in brown, green and grey, applied randomly for a mottled effect. Apply the colours first, then blend them using a damp paintbrush and allow the fabric to dry. Templates for the stones can be found on page 172; alternatively, simply cut them out by eye in a variety of shapes and sizes. You will need fifty to sixty stones altogether.

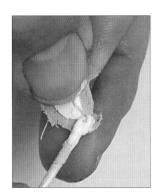

1 Cut each stone shape from thin card, then place it on the back of the painted calico and cut around it leaving a 2mm (¹/₁₆in) border.

2 Snip in to the calico, up to the edge of the card.

3 Apply PVA glue to the fabric using a cocktail stick and fold in the flaps.

4 When you have made enough stones, cut out the background for the wall from black card using the template provided on page 172 and glue them on. Lay the stones as close together as possible, as if you were building a real wall. Start on the right with the larger stones and gradually incorporate more smaller stones as you work towards the left. Alternatively, follow the pattern for the assembled wall on page 172.

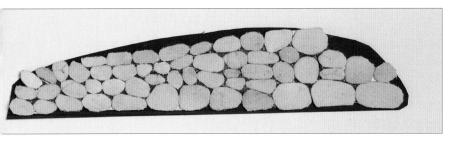

The finished wall.

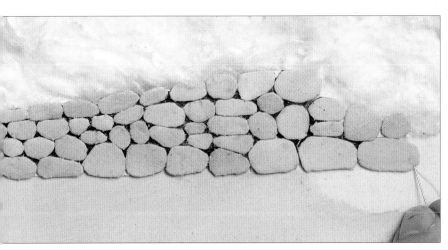

5 Trim off the excess card and attach the wall to your embroidery using stab stitching. Place the wall over the snow, not behind it.

6 Sew French knots and long stitches along the base of the wall to represent weeds. Use variegated brown-green cotton thread.

Tree

Make the tree on a separate piece of lightweight calico, measuring 305mm (12in) square. Using a brown watersoluble crayon, paint an area approximately 225 x 125mm (9 x 5in). When the paint is dry, transfer the outline for the tree using the template on page 170. Place the calico in a 255mm (10in) embroidery hoop.

1 Back stitch around the outline of the tree trunk and branches using two strands of brown six-stranded cotton and a No. 9 embroidery needle. Fill the trunk and branches using double Brussels stitch (see page 45), worked using two strands of variegated brown six-stranded cotton and a ballpoint needle. Start at the base of the trunk, and work up and down the tree in rows. Fill the leafy part of the tree with French knots (see page 30). Work some using two strands of brown six-stranded cotton and some with two strands of variegated brown-green cotton, using a No. 7 embroidery needle.

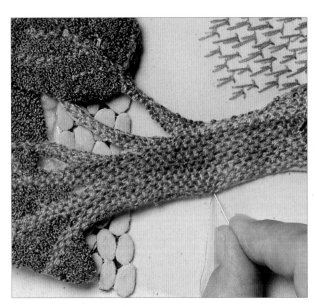

2 Cut out the slip for the tree leaving a 10mm (½in) margin and attach it to your embroidery using stab stitch. Place only a few securing stitches at the top of the tree so that it lies gently over the snow, and attach the trunk firmly using closely worked stitches.

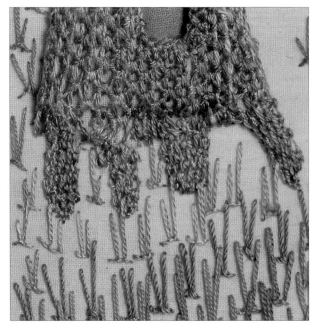

3 Working by eye, outline the tree roots using back stitch. Fill them using up and down stitch, as you did for the trunk. Add some more grass if necessary to blend the roots in with the background (see page 125).

Squirrel

The squirrel is made as two separate slips – one for the tail and one for the body. Templates for each are provided on page 172. Make the squirrel's body on a piece of lightweight calico and the tail on silk organza. The organza is finer than calico and lies more easily under the turkey knot stitching.

> **TIP**
>
> *Make the squirrel, deer and stag from the same piece of 205mm (8in) square lightweight calico mounted in a 150mm (6in) embroidery hoop.*

1 Embroider the top part of the body using a single strand of brown six-stranded cotton and a No. 9 embroidery needle. Change to a lighter brown for the middle part of the body and the front leg, and pale cream for the squirrel's chin and chest. Work in long and short stitch, starting at the nose and working backwards, following the curve of the body. To emphasise the back leg, change the direction of the stitches, working them up and down instead of across the shape. Sew on a black petite bead for the eye.

2 The tail is made using turkey knot stitch (see page 22). Work the loops in dense rows to make it soft and bushy.

3 Attach the squirrel's body close to the side of the tree using stab stitch, making sure that the surplus calico is tucked carefully underneath the body. Sew on the tail in the same way. For the ear, make a single chain stitch (consisting of a loop secured at the end with a small stitch) using two strands of cotton.

Deer

The deer is made on the same piece of lightweight calico as the squirrel and stag. The template is provided on page 170. Long and short stitch is used to fill the body, worked using a single strand of six-stranded cotton and a No. 9 embroidery needle. To give the impression of fur, pass each stitch through the middle of the stitch above for a slightly irregular finish.

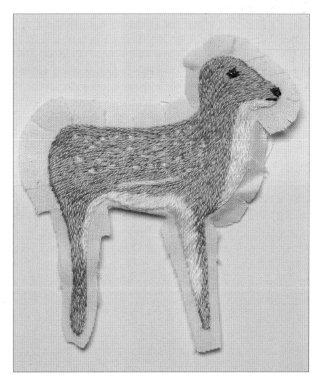

1 Begin by embroidering the cream-coloured markings on the deer's body. Use satin stitch for the spots and stem stitch for the line. Starting at the nose, work the head, neck, body and legs in long and short stitch, following the contours of the body. Use light brown thread for the main parts of the deer, and pale cream for the underside and inner parts of the legs. Finish by sewing on the eye, nose and mouth using satin stitch worked with a single thread of black six-stranded cotton.

2 Embroider the legs on the background fabric using long and short stitch, first checking that they align correctly with the completed slip. Work the tops of the legs in light brown and the lower parts in pale cream. Add more grass to help them blend with the background.

3 Attach the deer to the background following the method described on page 117. Cut two ears from a piece of light brown gloving leather using the template provided and glue them in place using PVA glue. Use tweezers to help position them.

Stag

Make the stag in the same way as the deer, on the same piece of calico. Start by embroidering the spots and line along the side of the body using a single strand of pale cream six-stranded cotton and a No. 9 embroidery needle. Work the spots in satin stitch and the line in stem stitch. Return to the nose, and fill the head with long and short stitch worked from the nose outwards using a light brown thread. For the body and legs, work right to left, following the body's contours, using light brown for the main parts, and cream for the deer's chest, belly and the lower parts of its front leg. Finally, use satin stitch worked in a single black thread for the eyes and nose, and stem stitch for the shading under the head and the tail.

After completing the stag, cut it out from the calico and make sure it fits over the two legs outlined on the background. Embroider these two legs using long and short stitch. Attach the stag to the background fabric, turning the surplus material underneath as you work (see page 117).

Antlers

Though not worked in needlelace, the easiest way to make the antlers is on a needlelace pad. The templates are provided on page 170.

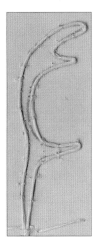
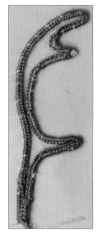
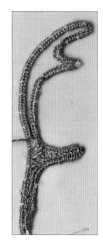

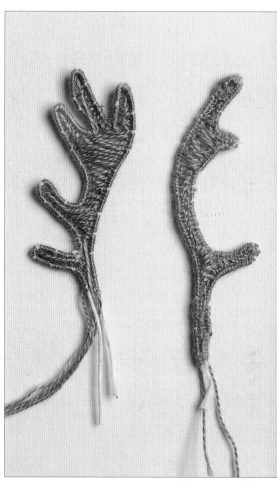

1 Couch a length of paper-covered wire over the design using white sewing cotton. Leave a tail of at least 25mm (1in).

2 Work buttonhole stitches over the wire, with the loops on the inside of the shape. Use a single strand of dark brown cotton and a ballpoint needle.

3 Make satin stitches across the shape, passing the thread through the buttonhole stitches on either side. Leave long tail threads.

The completed antler.

4 Complete both antlers and remove them from the needlelace pad.

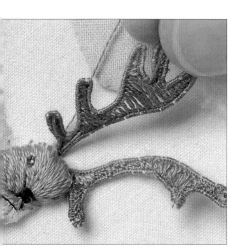

5 Insert the antlers through two holes made in the fabric using a darning needle. Pass the tail threads and wires through to the back of the work and use the threads to oversew the antlers in place.

6 Complete the stag by adding two ears, cut from light brown gloving leather using the templates on page 170.

Summer

This delightful scene covers the lower part of the embroidery, and includes a number of elements worked in needlelace, a traditional technique that has been used in stumpwork for hundreds of years. The swan, fish and frog are made entirely of needlelace, and the heron and wader are made of gloving leather, with needlelace wings. The picture is framed by the yellow needlelace irises on the left and the pink lily on the right. We have used machine stitching on the iris leaves, but the same finish can be achieved by hand stitching if you do not have access to a sewing machine. Rocks and ferns border the pond, and mark the transition from spring to summer, and from summer to autumn.

The irises are composed of three different types of petal, and involve some new techniques that have not been used elsewhere: we show you how to change to a different colour thread, how to work with two needles, and how to create ring picots.

Materials

- Sewing machine (optional)
- 150mm (6in) embroidery hoop and 255mm (10in) embroidery hoop
- Silk frame, 255mm (10in) square, and pins
- Embroidery, general-purpose and large scissors
- Nos. 7 and 9 embroidery needle, No. 9 sharps needle, two No. 9 ballpoint needles and a darning needle
- Berry-head and lace pins
- Full-size templates for the wader, fish, heron, swan, frog and iris leaves
- Needlelace pads for the iris petals, wader's wing, swan, swan's wing, fish, frog, lily and heron's wing
- Two pieces of silk organza, 610 x 305mm (24 x 12in) and 205mm (8in) square
- White felt, 305mm (12in) square
- White gloving leather, 130 x 75mm (5 x 3in)
- Six-stranded cotton in black, pink, pale green, orange, white, yellow and dark brown
- Variegated six-stranded cotton in light blue, greens, browns and reds
- 100/3 fine silk thread in yellow, white, orange, black, grey, light blue and mid-brown
- Sewing cotton
- Fine copper wire
- Paper-covered wire
- Black acrylic paint
- Green fabric paint
- Watersoluble crayons in green and brown
- Three paintbrushes (fine, medium and large)
- Gold gel pen
- PVA glue
- Two black and one silver petite beads
- Black seed bead
- Pressed-paper egg boxes
- Tweezers
- Surgical tape

Rocks and irises

The freestanding irises are made of needlelace, and the patterns for these are provided on page 162. The templates for the leaves are on page 170. You can make as many flowers as you wish, though we found that four worked well. The leaves are made from green-painted silk organza, outlined in machine stitch, though back stitching by hand would work just as well.

You will need about twelve rocks altogether. Make them from pieces of pressed-paper egg box, following the method described on page 136.

Rocks

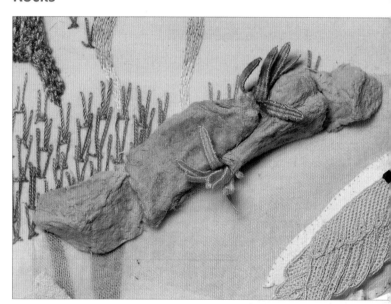

Attach four rocks at the side of the pond using stab stitch. Insert some ferns (see page 134) into the crevices, as on page 136.

Iris leaves

Begin by painting a piece of silk organza measuring 610 x 305mm (24 x 12in) using green fabric paint. Allow the silk to dry.

1 Fold the green-painted organza in half to make a piece 610 x 150mm (24 x 6in) and place part of it in a 255mm (10in) hoop. Leave enough spare fabric to make two more sets of leaves. Transfer the design using one of the templates provided and sew around the outline in green sewing cotton using either machine stitching or back stitching. Repeat this twice more, making three sets of double-thickness leaves.

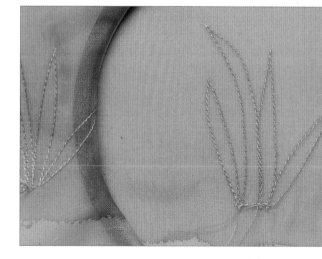

151

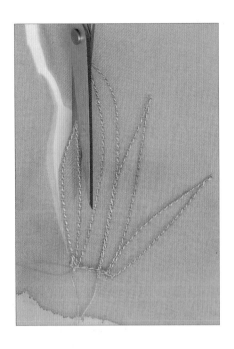

2 Take the fabric out of the hoop and cut around the leaf outlines using a pair of sharp scissors. Cut as close to the stitching as possible.

3 Attach one set of iris leaves to the embroidery, just below the base of the tree. Stab stitch along the base of the leaves only.

Iris flowers

The filling stitch for the iris petals is corded single Brussels stitch. A fine wire is incorporated into the cordonnets leaving 50mm (2in) tails, and each petal is top stitched around the edge (see page 43). There are three different types of petal, and you will need to make three of each for each flower. All the petals for each flower can be made on the same needlelace pad. Use a single strand of 100/3 fine silk and a ballpoint needle. The centres of the large petals have been worked with a deeper, orange silk thread. Full instructions on changing to a different-coloured thread are given on the facing page.

The edges of the middle-sized petals are decorated with four ring picots. Instructions for these are provided right.

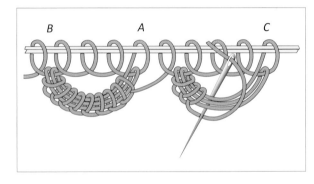

Ring picots

Working from the left, top stitch around the edge of the shape to A. Take the needle and thread back under the buttonhole stitch at B to form a loop. Make another loop back to A, and a third back to B. You now have three threads in the loop. Buttonhole over these three threads until you get back to A. Continue top stitching to C and repeat.

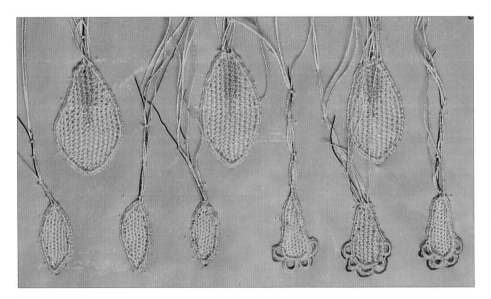

The completed petals for one of the irises, before releasing them from the needlelace pad. We made four irises altogether.

Changing thread colour

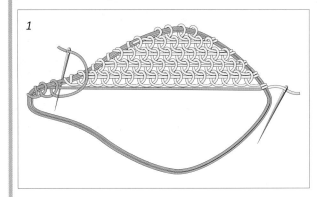

1 Work the yellow filling stitches down to the point where you want to change colour. Take the thread twice around the cordonnet. Leave the thread on the needle. Pass the orange thread through a second needle, and join it to the cordonnet on the right-hand side. Lay the thread across the shape and loop it twice around the cordonnet on the other side. Work as many orange stitches as you need into the previous row, picking up the orange cord.

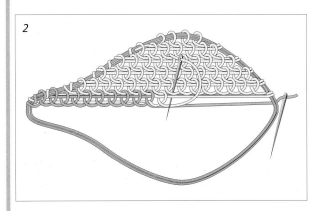

2 When you have made enough orange stitches, lay the thread across the row and under the cordonnet. Leave the needle on the thread. Pick up the needle with the yellow thread and lay the thread across the shape, taking it behind the orange stitches. Wrap the thread twice around the cordonnet on the left-hand side and bring it to the front through the last orange stitch worked. Work yellow stitches to the end of the row, picking up the yellow cord only.

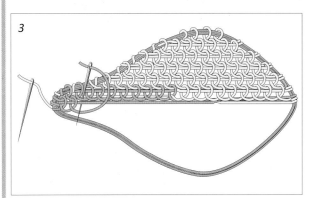

3 Take both needles under and over the cordonnet, lay both threads back across the shape and secure. In the next row, work as many stitches as you need with the orange thread over the orange cord.

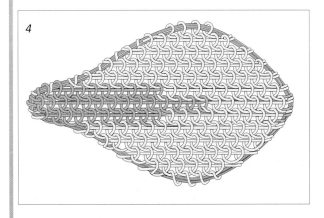

4 Pick up the yellow thread and continue across the shape working over the yellow cord. Take both needles under and over the cordonnet, lay both threads back across the shape and secure. In the next row, work as many orange stitches as you need over the orange cord. Pick up the needle with the yellow thread, bring it to the front, going through the last stitch worked, and continue across the shape. Work over the yellow cord. Finish off the orange cord by running it under some of the couching stitches on the right-hand side. Continue filling the shape with the yellow thread.

5 Bind together the three inner (smallest) petals with their top sides facing outwards. Use a single strand of green six-stranded cotton wrapped around the tops of the stems, just below the petals.

6 Using the same thread, bind in the middle-sized petals.

7 Bind in the outer petals, taking the green thread 30mm (1¼in) down the stem. Using tweezers, bend the outer and middle petals downwards, then turn the middle petals upwards at their tips.

8 Lay two irises over the first set of leaves and oversew them in place at the bases of their stems. Attach another set of leaves over the top, then the remaining two irises, and finally the third set of leaves.

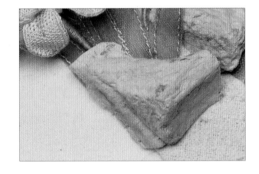

9 Attach one or two of the rocks you made earlier (see page 151) around the base of the irises.

Heron

The heron is made of gloving leather, with three layers of felt padding underneath. The templates are provided on page 171. The wing is made of needlelace, the pattern for which is given on page 164, together with detailed instructions on how to make the cordonnet on page 165.

1 Attach the three layers of padding, following the instructions on page 116.

2 Cut out the shape for the heron's body from white gloving leather and pin it in place over the padding. Position the pins at the edge of the leather, where there will eventually be stitches.

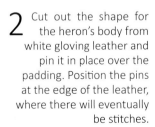

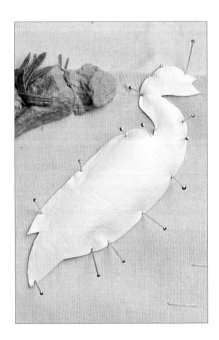

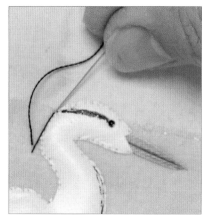

TIP

Always pin the elements in place first to ensure they are positioned correctly before stitching them.

3 Use small, neat stab stitches to secure the heron's body using white silk thread. Place stitches in the holes left by the pins so that the holes do not show. For the beak, make six long satin stitches with a single strand of orange six-stranded cotton, and one long stitch in black cotton. Attach a single black petite bead using black thread for the eye. The black markings down the front of the heron's body and on its head are drawn on using acrylic paint and a fine paintbrush.

4 Add two straight stitches, using a single strand of black cotton, to make the long, black plume on the back of the heron's head.

5 For the heron's leg, cut a 100mm (4in) length of paper-covered wire and fold it in half. Using the fine paintbrush, apply a small amount of PVA glue to one end to secure the thread, then tightly wrap the wire with pale green six-stranded cotton; leave the last 10mm (½in) bare. Wind some white cotton thread around the top of the leg. Knot each thread to finish, and cut them off leaving a long tail.

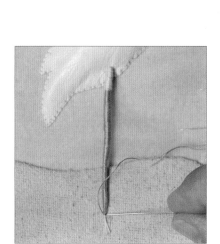

6 Lay the top of the leg over the heron's body and use the tail threads to attach the leg at the top and bottom with two or three securing stitches (the bottom of the leg will eventually be hidden under a rock).

7 Make the needlelace wing using 100/3 fine silk thread in black and grey, and a ballpoint needle. The filling stitch is corded single Brussels stitch. Follow the instructions on page 165 for the cordonnet. Attach it to the heron, using the tail threads, with two or three holding stitches spaced evenly along the top edge.

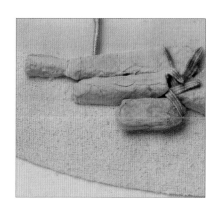

8 Place some more rocks and a fern (see page 151) around the base of the heron to cover up the bottom of the leg.

Swan

Like the heron, the swan has three layers of padding, for which templates are provided on page 171. The swan's body, however, is made of needlelace. The filling stitch used is corded single Brussels stitch, worked with two needles. The wing feathers are made as a single piece of needlelace, using the same filling stitch and worked in the same thread as the body. A thin wire is incorporated into the cordonnet to allow the wing to stand proud of the body, and top stitching applied to define the feathers. The needlelace patterns are provided on page 163, along with instructions for making the cordonnets.

1 Cut out the three layers of padding for the swan and attach them following the method described on page 116.

2 Make the swan's body using white 100/3 fine silk thread and two No. 9 ballpoint needles. Instructions for working with two needles are provided below. Pin the needlelace in place over the padding, then secure it with stab stitches worked evenly around the outside. Attach a black petite bead using a single black cotton thread for the eye.

Making the swan's body, using two needles

Attach a white thread at A (see above) and work a foundation row of buttonhole stitches along the bottom edge and up the neck to B. Lay the thread back to A and take it under the cordonnet, but do not secure it. Leave the thread on the needle. Attach a second thread to the cordonnet and work into the loops of the preceding row, picking up the loose cord thread (see Diagram 1).

Work to the end of the row. Lay the thread back across the row, and take it under the cordonnet but do not secure it. Pick up the first needle, carefully adjust the thread tension, take it round the cordonnet once and work the row in the same way as the previous one (see Diagram 2).

Continue working with the two needles until you reach the cordonnet at C. The neck should now be complete, leaving just the swan's back to be filled. Complete the swan's body using a single needle and thread.

Make the beak, and the black marking behind the beak, using single strands of orange and black silk thread respectively. Use corded single Brussels stitch, as for the body.

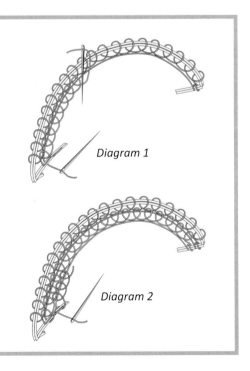

Diagram 1

Diagram 2

3 Make the wing using the same filling stitch as the body, and working in the same thread. Incorporate a thin wire into the cordonnet, and apply top stitching around the outside of the wing and along the edges of the feathers. Pin the wing in place, and attach it by stitching around the base, from A to B.

The completed swan.

Wader

The wader is made in the same way as the heron. Begin by attaching two layers of felt padding (see page 116), then the body, which is cut from soft gloving leather. Templates for all these shapes can be found on page 170.

The legs are paper-covered wire wrapped in a single strand of orange six-stranded cotton. Bend them into shape, and attach them in the same way as the heron's leg on page 155. Once in place, stitch on three small straight stitches at the end of each leg for feet. For the beak, make four long satin stitches with a single strand of black six-stranded cotton, and for the eye sew a single French knot using the same black thread.

Make a needlelace wing using the pattern supplied on page 162. The filling stitch is corded single Brussels stitch, worked using one strand of black 100/3 fine silk and a ballpoint needle. Apply top stitching around the cordonnet, incorporating a fine copper wire as you do so to strengthen the edge of the wing. Sew the wing to the wader's body by stab stitching along the top edge.

157

Fish

The fish is a piece of needlelace and is simple to make. The pattern is provided on page 164, along with instructions on how to construct the cordonnet. It is worked in corded single Brussels stitch using a single strand of variegated light blue six-stranded cotton and a ballpoint needle. The fish is attached to the background over a single layer of padding, with the lower half of its body under the blue-painted chiffon, suggesting it is jumping out of the water.

1 Make the needlelace fish. Sew a silver petite bead on to the head for an eye using one strand of blue six-stranded cotton. The two bottom fins are needle-woven picots. Follow the instructions on page 174, attaching the base of each picot to the cordonnet by passing the needle and thread through the couching stitches. Top stitch the tail and top fin, incorporating a thin copper wire underneath the top stitching on the fin. Leave two tails of wire, approximately 25mm (1in) long.

2 Make a small, horizontal slit in the chiffon, along the gold line drawn on to the background fabric. Cut out the felt padding, slide it halfway under the chiffon and stab stitch the top part in place.

3 Position the needlelace fish over the padding, with the lower half of the fish under the chiffon, and stab stitch the upper half in place.

Frog

The needlelace frog is made in three parts – the body, the front leg and the back leg. The patterns and instructions for the cordonnet are provided on page 164. Use corded single Brussels stitch worked with one strand of variegated brown six-stranded cotton. The frog's toes have no filling stitches between the cordonnet threads; when the leg is attached to the background fabric, sew the three loops in position to look like toes.

Begin by sewing the two layers of felt padding, see page 172, on to the background fabric – the double layer under the frog's head serves to bring it level with the raised area of grass.

1 Attach the needlelace for the frog's body over the padding, adding small French knots for the spots, worked using a single strand of dark brown six-stranded cotton and a No. 7 embroidery needle, and a tiny black seed bead for the eye. Cut a small sliver of felt slightly smaller than the frog's front leg, and attach it to the frog's body, then sew the front leg over the padding.

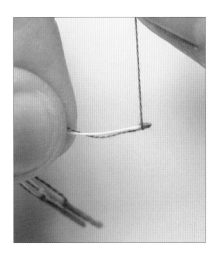

2 To make the frog's back foot, cut three lengths of paper-covered wire, each 80mm (3¼in) long. Dip the tip of each one in PVA glue and wrap the first 10mm (½in) with a single strand of dark brown six-stranded cotton.

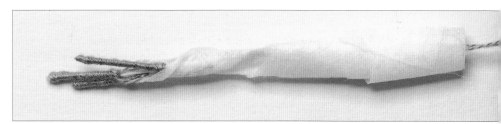

3 Bind the three lengths of wire together loosely with surgical tape to create the frog's back leg. Taper the leg from the upper part to the ankle.

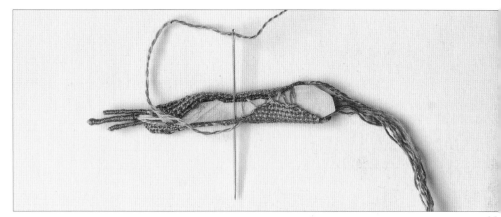

4 Wrap the needlelace around the leg, and lace the two edges together on the back using one strand of variegated brown six-stranded cotton.

5 Tuck in all the tail threads, and make two bends in the leg: one at the knee and one at the ankle.

6 Pin the back leg in place, and secure it around the upper part only, using stab stitches.

Lily and lily pads

Make the lily pads and lily using the patterns and instructions provided
on pages 164–165. Detailed instructions for the lily pads are given in the
needlelace section, on pages 118–121. Use a single strand of variegated
green six-stranded cotton. The filling stitch used for the flower is corded
single Brussels stitch, made using a single strand of pink six-stranded cotton.
A fine wire is couched around the outside of each petal with the cordonnet
threads, and then top stitching applied to give a raised edge.

*The three complete
lily pads. Leave
long tail threads for
sewing them to the
background fabric.*

*The completed parts
for the lily.*

1 Attach each lily pad using just three or four stab stitches to hold them in place.

2 Lay on the outer background petals of the lily and secure them with two or three stab stitches around the base.

3 Secure the inner petals in the same way. Take the wires through to the back of the fabric, and bend the petals inwards towards the centre of the flower.

4 Make the stamens in the centre of the flower using turkey knot stitch (see page 22). Sew them in a row along the base of the petals. Use three strands of yellow six-stranded cotton and a No. 9 embroidery needle.

5 Attach the four larger of the individual petals in a row along the base of the flower. Twist the two end wires of each petal together first, then make a hole in the fabric with a darning needle and pass the wires through to the other side. Take the tail threads through to the back of your work and use them to overstitch the wires in place. Bend the petals outwards, away from the centre of the flower.

TIP

When arranging the petals on the background fabric, follow the numbered diagram on page 164.

6 Attach the three smaller individual petals just within the outer ones, using the same method to secure them. Bend these petals up towards the centre of the flower. Arrange all the petals to give a pleasing, three-dimensional shape to the lily.

Needlelace patterns for the seasons

The following needlelace patterns are all reproduced full size. Trace the patterns on to white paper, and use the tracings to make the needlelace pads (see page 118). The arrows on the diagrams indicate the direction of working.

Most of the cordonnets are fairly straightforward and require no explanation; for the more complicated ones, detailed instructions and a diagram are provided.

TIP

The sizes of the patterns provided in this book are for the needlelace we made; yours may differ in size or tension. Always check that your needlelace is the right size for your embroidery, and adjust the size or tension as necessary.

Small fir tree, page 129.

Cordonnet for the small fir tree
Start with a loop at A and couch both threads round the top of the tree to B. At B, take one thread to C, couching it down in a few places to keep it on the design line. Make a loop and couch both threads back to B. Continue couching both threads to D, then repeat the method above for D to E. Continue round to F, and repeat again for F to G. Finally couch both threads back to A and finish in the normal way.

Large fir tree, page 129.

Iris petals, page 152.

Wader's wing, page 157.

Snowdrop petals, page 127.

162

Blossom petals,
page 138.

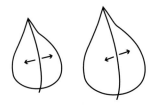

Large and small blossom leaves,
and catkin leaves, pages 138 and 140.

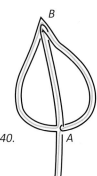

Cordonnet for the blossom and catkin leaves

Each leaf has a fine wire (shown in orange) incorporated into the cordonnet. Make a loop in the thread at A. Starting 25mm (1in) from the end of the wire, couch the two threads and the wire round the outside of the leaf until you get back to A. Take one of the threads and the wire up the central vein to B. Loop the thread under the couched threads, and lay it back down to A. Cut off the surplus wire, and couch down both threads and the wire back to A. Pass one thread through the loop at A, and leave two tail threads of 25mm (1in).

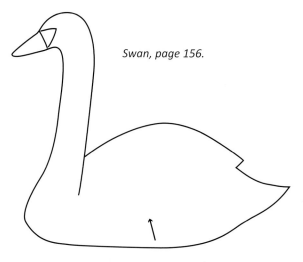

Swan, page 156.

Dragonfly's wings, page 127.

Cordonnet for the swan

Start with a loop at A and couch both threads round to B. Take one thread down to C and form a loop. Couch both threads back to B, pick up the thread you left behind, and continue couching both threads round to D. Take one of the threads up to E, couching it down in a few places to keep it on the design line. Make a loop around the cordonnet at E, and couch both threads back to D. Loop the thread over and under the cordonnet, and take it back to E via F, again couching it down in a few places to keep it on the design line. Make another loop at E, and couch both threads back to D via F. Pick up the other thread and couch round the rest of the shape to A. Finish in the normal way.

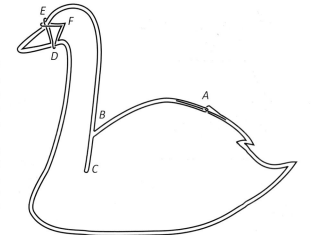

Swan's wing, page
156.

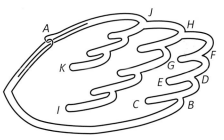

Cordonnet for the swan's wing

Start with a loop at A and couch both threads round the base of the wing to B. Take one thread to C, make a loop and couch both threads back to B. Continue round to D, and repeat for D to E, then F to G. Couch the threads round to H, then take one thread down to I, making the loops on the way back to H. Repeat for J to K. Finally couch both threads back to A and finish in the normal way.

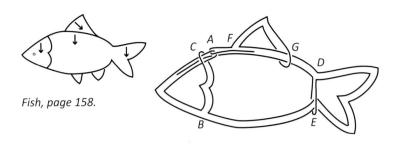

Fish, page 158.

Cordonnet for the fish

Start with a loop at A, and couch both threads round the fish's nose to B. Take one thread across to C, couching it down in a few places to keep it on the design line. At C, take the thread over and under the cordonnet and couch both threads back to B. Continue round to D, take one thread down to E, loop it round the cordonnet as before, and couch both threads back to D. Continue round to F, and take one thread back to G. Put an extra couching stitch at the tip of the fin to hold it in place. Loop the thread around the cordonnet, and couch both threads back to F. Pick up the other thread and continue to A, finishing in the normal way.

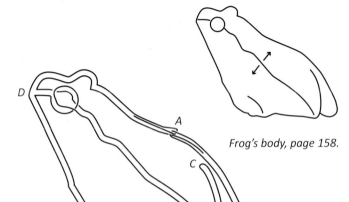

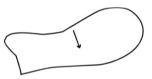

Frog's body, page 158.

Frog's back leg, page 158.

Frog's front leg, page 158.

Cordonnet for the frog's body

Start with a loop at A and couch both threads round to B. Take one thread up to C, couching it down in a few places to keep it on the design line, make a loop, and couch both threads back to B. Continue couching round to D. Take one thread down to B, going round the eye one-and-a-half times. Loop the thread under and over the cordonnet at B and couch both threads back to D, taking the working thread round the side of the eye that has only one thread. Continue round to A and finish in the normal way.

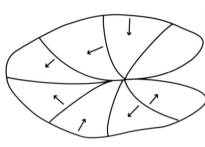

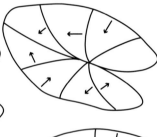

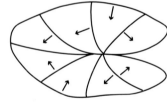

Lily pads, page 160.

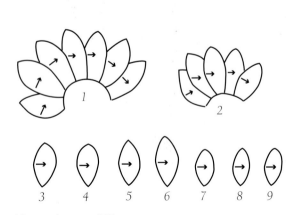

Lily petals, page 160.

Arrangement of lily petals, page 161.

Heron's wing, page 155.

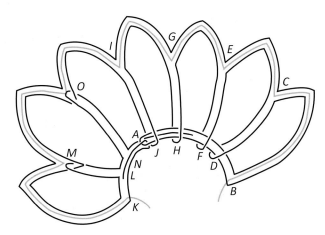

Cordonnet for the lily background petals

Start with a loop at A and couch both threads round to B. Add a fine wire (shown in orange), and couch both threads and the wire round to C. Leave a 25mm (1in) tail of wire. Take one thread down to D, couching it down in a few places to keep it on the design line, loop it under and over the cordonnet and couch both threads back to C. Pick up the wire and the thread you left behind, and couch both threads and the wire round to E. Repeat the method above for E to F, G to H and I to J. From I, couch both threads and the wire round to K. Leave the wire at K, and couch both threads to L. Take one thread up to M, loop it round the cordonnet and couch both threads back to L. Take both threads to N, and repeat for N to O. From N, couch both threads to A and finish in the normal way. Cut off the wire, leaving a 25mm (1in) tail.

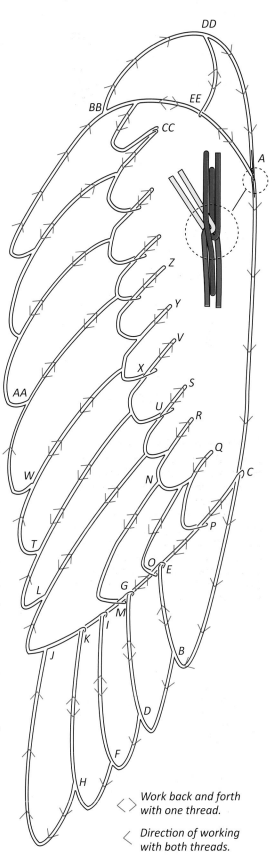

Cordonnet for the heron's wing

Cut a length of thread approximately 760mm (30in) long. Make a loop about 200mm (7¾in) from one end and start couching at A. Couch both threads down until you get to B. Make a branch by taking the longest thread round to C via E, couching it down in a few places to hold it on the design line. Loop the thread over and under the cordonnet, and couch both threads back to B. Continue round to D, and make further branches from D to E, F to G and H to I. From H, couch both threads to J. Take one thread to K, loop it round the cordonnet, and couch both threads back to J. Continue round to L. Take one thread round to M via N, couching it down on the design line at regular intervals. At M, loop the thread round the cordonnet and couch down both threads back to N. Repeat the process down to O, and then to P. From P, work up to Q, put a loop in the thread and secure the loop with a couching stitch, and continue round to R, then S, and back down to L where you can pick up the thread you left behind. Couch both threads to T, branch off to U, then round to V. Put in a loop at V, secured with a single couching stitch, and couch both threads back to T. Couch round to W, then branch off at X, Y and Z, with loops at Y and Z. Couch both threads to AA and work the next three feathers in the same way, until you get to BB. Take one thread to CC, loop it round the cordonnet and continue along to A and back to BB. Continue couching both threads to DD, take one thread to EE and back to DD, then carry on round to A to complete the cordonnet. Finish as shown on the diagram.

⟨ ⟩ Work back and forth with one thread.

⟨ Direction of working with both threads.

165

Templates

The templates on the following pages are either full-size or half-size.
The half-size templates need to be enlarged to 200 per cent to make
a full-size template using a photocopier. The full-size templates can
be photocopied or traced on to tracing paper.

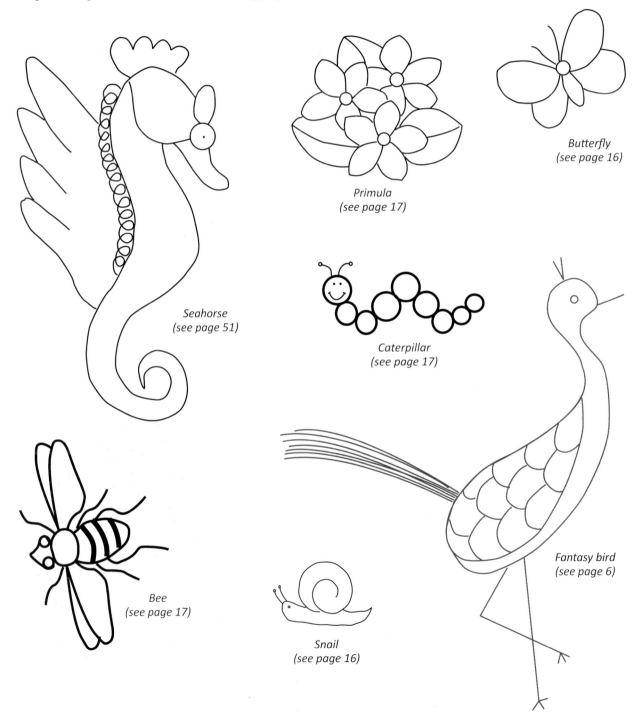

*Seahorse
(see page 51)*

*Primula
(see page 17)*

*Butterfly
(see page 16)*

*Caterpillar
(see page 17)*

*Bee
(see page 17)*

*Snail
(see page 16)*

*Fantasy bird
(see page 6)*

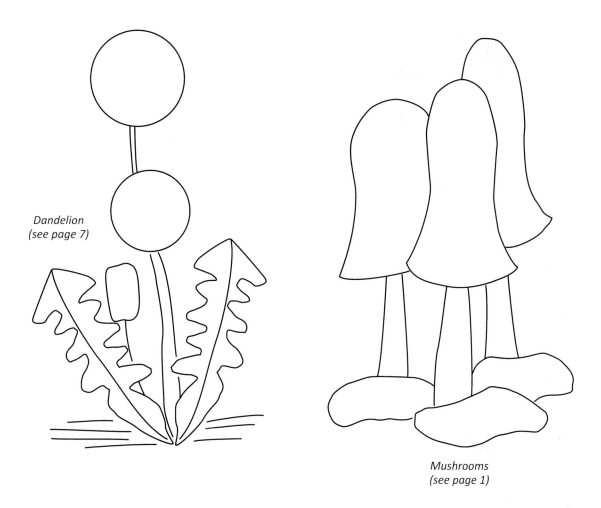

*Dandelion
(see page 7)*

*Mushrooms
(see page 1)*

Templates for the figures

All the templates for the figures are reproduced full size. From these you can derive patterns for the body parts, padding and clothes.

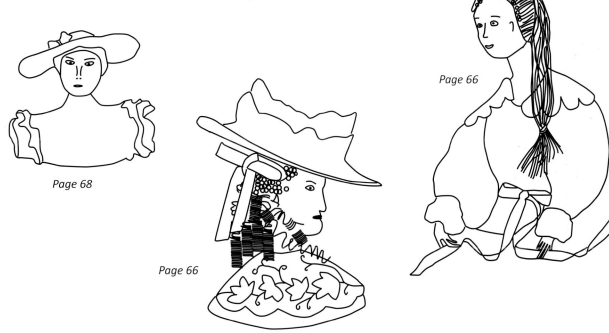

Page 68

Page 66

Page 66

Page 67

Page 3

Page 81

Page 66

Templates for the seasons embroidery

For elements that need to be embroidered before being attached to the main embroidery, for example the deer and stag, make a full-size copy of the template, place it underneath the fabric, and trace around the outline using a gold gel pen. Work in a well-lit area, over a lightbox if possible.

For elements that simply need to be cut out and attached to the main embroidery, such as felt padding, and the water and grass shown below, cut out a full-size version of the template, pin it to the fabric and cut round it.

The log cabin and the fence should be photocopied and cut out, glued or simply laid on to the centre of a piece of A4 paper, and then photocopied again. The cabin and the fence are then constructed by laying the components over the equivalent parts of the template on the A4 sheet.

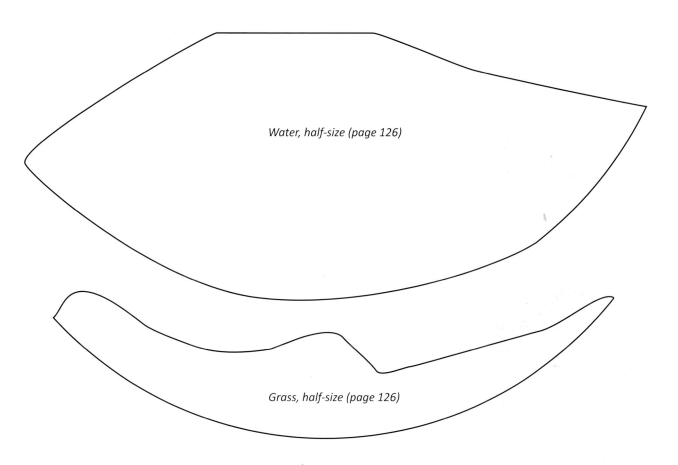

Water, half-size (page 126)

Grass, half-size (page 126)

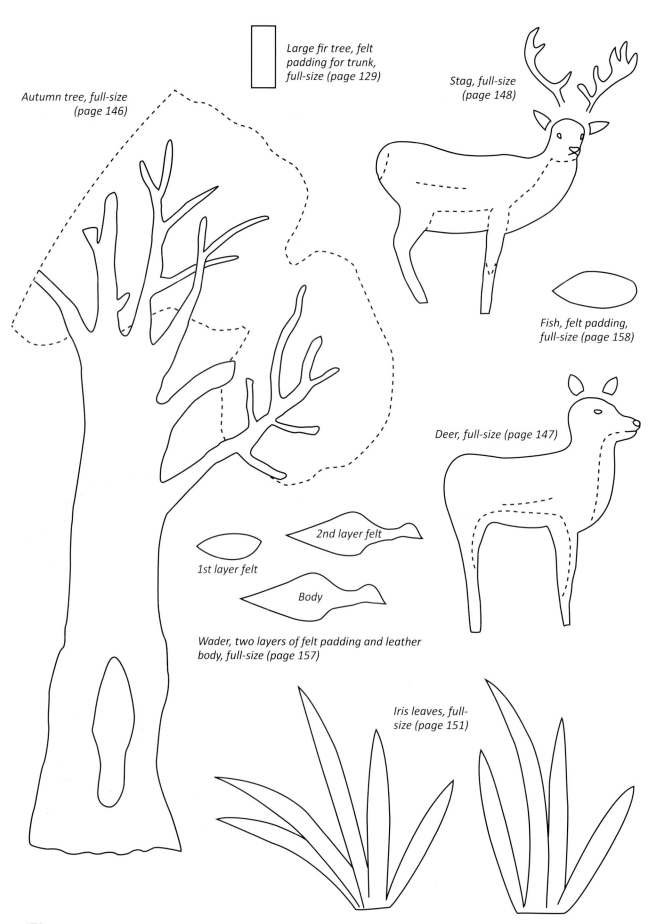

Large fir tree, felt padding for trunk, full-size (page 129)

Stag, full-size (page 148)

Autumn tree, full-size (page 146)

Fish, felt padding, full-size (page 158)

Deer, full-size (page 147)

2nd layer felt

1st layer felt

Body

Wader, two layers of felt padding and leather body, full-size (page 157)

Iris leaves, full-size (page 151)

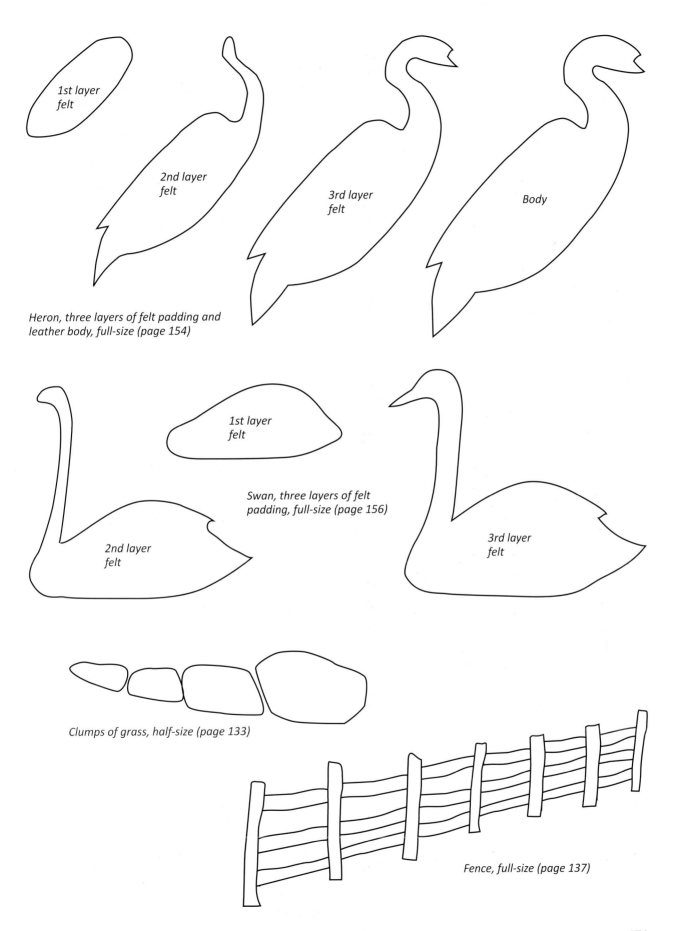

1st layer
felt

2nd layer
felt

3rd layer
felt

Body

Heron, three layers of felt padding and
leather body, full-size (page 154)

1st layer
felt

2nd layer
felt

3rd layer
felt

Swan, three layers of felt
padding, full-size (page 156)

Clumps of grass, half-size (page 133)

Fence, full-size (page 137)

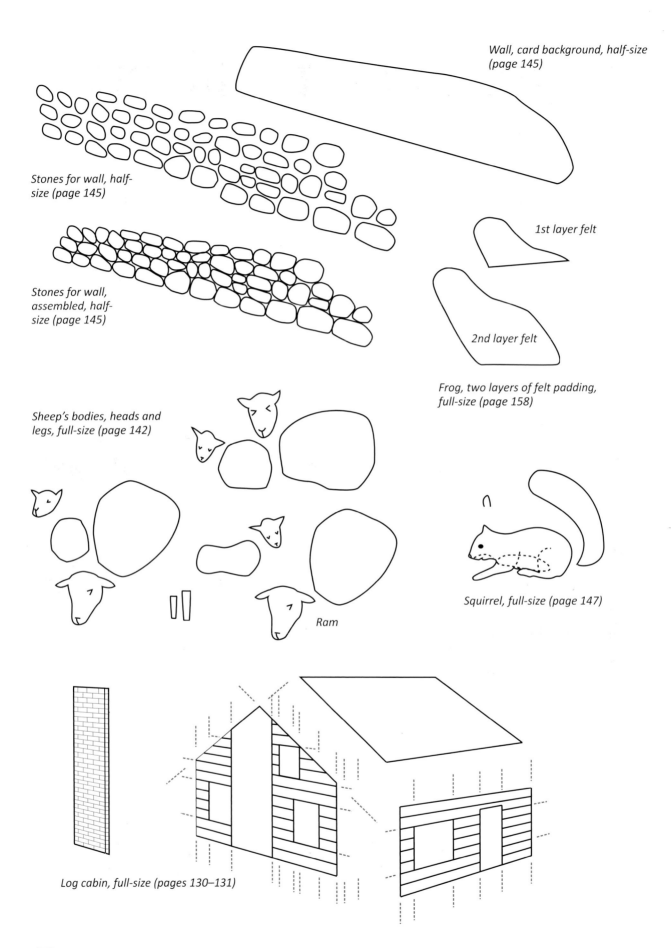

Wall, card background, half-size
(page 145)

Stones for wall, half-size (page 145)

Stones for wall, assembled, half-size (page 145)

1st layer felt

2nd layer felt

Frog, two layers of felt padding, full-size (page 158)

Sheep's bodies, heads and legs, full-size (page 142)

Ram

Squirrel, full-size (page 147)

Log cabin, full-size (pages 130–131)

Embroidery stitch library

All of the embroidery stitches used in the book are shown in the following diagrams.

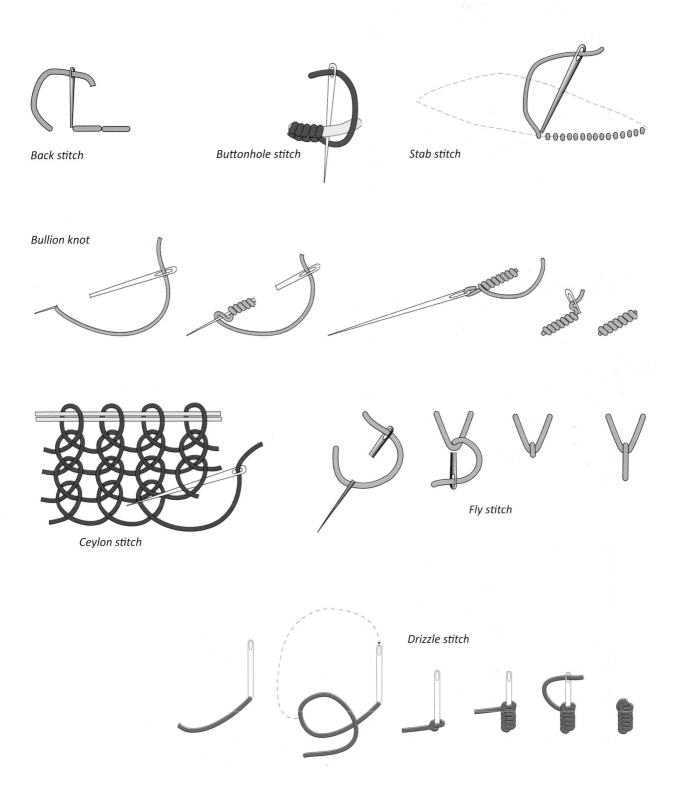

Back stitch

Buttonhole stitch

Stab stitch

Bullion knot

Ceylon stitch

Fly stitch

Drizzle stitch

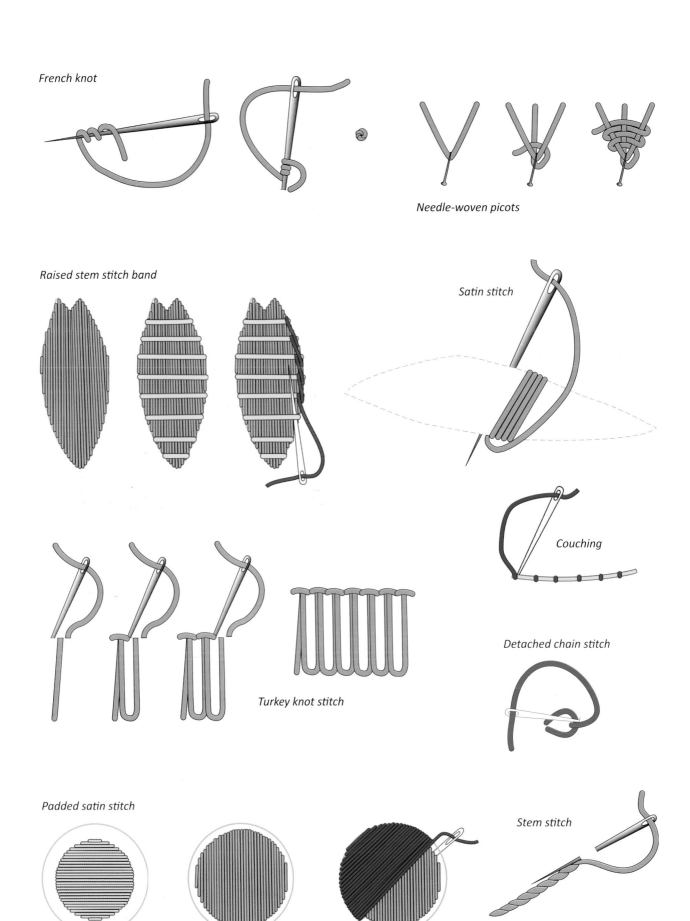

French knot

Needle-woven picots

Raised stem stitch band

Satin stitch

Couching

Turkey knot stitch

Detached chain stitch

Padded satin stitch

Stem stitch

174

Padded raised chain band stitch

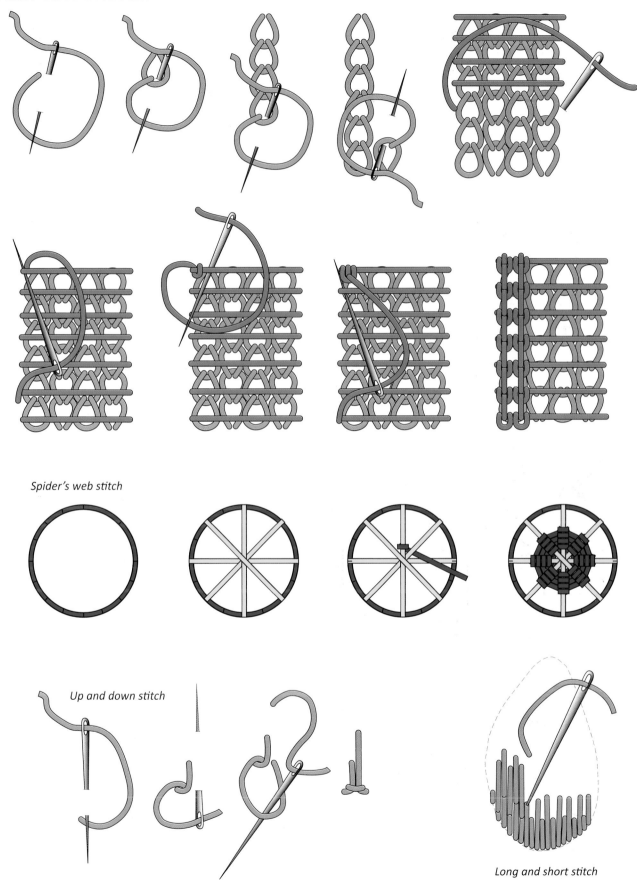

Spider's web stitch

Up and down stitch

Long and short stitch

Index